COACHING YOUTH

FOOTBALL

SECOND EDITION

American Sport Education Program

Human Kinetics

Library of Congress Cataloging-in-Publication Data

Coaching youth football/ American Sport Education Program. -- 2nd ed.
    p. cm.
    Rev. ed. of: Rookie coaches football guide. c1993.
    ISBN 0-88011-539-4
    1. Youth league football--Coaching.   I. American Sport Education
Program.   II. Rookie coaches football guide.
GV956.6.R66   1997
796.332'07'7--dc20   96-31306
                                                       CIP

ISBN: 0-88011-539-4

This book is the second edition of *Rookie Coaches Football Guide*.

Acquisitions Editor: Jim Kestner; **Flag and Touch Football Consultant:** Michael Cihon, United States Flag and Touch Football League; **Developmental Editor:** Jan Colarusso Seeley; **Assistant Editors:** Erin Cler, Lynn M. Hooper, Coree Schutter; **Copyeditor:** Bob Replinger; **Proofreader:** Jim Burns; **Graphic Designer:** Judy Henderson; **Graphic Artist:** Francine Hamerski; **Cover Designer:** Stuart Cartwright; **Photographer (cover):** Anthony Neste; **Illustrators:** Paul To and Tim Offenstein, line drawings; and Studio 2D, Mac art; **Printer:** United Graphics

Printed in the United States of America   10 9 8 7 6 5 4 3 2

Human Kinetics
Web site: http://www.humankinetics.com/

United States: Human Kinetics, P.O. Box 5076, Champaign, IL 61825-5076
1-800-747-4457
e-mail: humank@hkusa.com

Canada: Human Kinetics, Box 24040, Windsor, ON N8Y 4Y9
1-800-465-7301 (in Canada only)
e-mail: humank@hkcanada.com

Europe: Human Kinetics, P.O. Box IW14, Leeds LS16 6TR, United Kingdom
(44) 1132 781708
e-mail: humank@hkeurope.com

Australia: Human Kinetics, 57A Price Avenue, Lower Mitcham, South Australia 5062
(088) 277 1555
e-mail: humank@hkaustralia.com

New Zealand: Human Kinetics, P.O. Box 105-231, Auckland 1
(09) 523 3462
e-mail: humank@hknewz.com

Contents

Welcome to Coaching!

Coaching young people is an exciting way to be involved in sport. But it isn't easy. Some coaches are overwhelmed by the responsibilities involved in helping athletes through their early sport experiences. And that's not surprising, because coaching youngsters requires more than bringing the footballs and equipment to the field and letting them play. It involves preparing them physically and mentally to compete effectively, fairly, and safely in their sport, and providing them with a positive role model.

This book will help you meet the challenges *and* experience the many rewards of coaching young athletes. We call it *Coaching Youth Football* because it is intended for adults with little or no formal preparation in coaching football. In this book you'll learn how to apply general coaching principles and teach football rules, skills, and strategies successfully to kids. And while you may find that some of the information does not apply to your amateur football program, we're confident this book will help you get a good jump on your coaching career.

The American Sport Education Program (ASEP) thanks Mike Cihon of the United States Flag and Touch Football League and Pop Warner Little Scholars for contributing their football expertise to this book. Combined with ASEP's material on important coaching principles, this book covers all the bases.

This book also serves as a text for ASEP's Rookie Coaches Course. If you would like more information about this course or ASEP, please contact us at

ASEP
P.O. Box 5076
Champaign, IL 61825-5076
(800) 747-5698

Good Coaching!

Unit 1

Who, Me . . .
a Coach?

If you are like most rookie coaches, you have probably been recruited from the ranks of concerned parents, sport enthusiasts, or community volunteers. And, like many rookie and veteran coaches, you probably have had little formal instruction on how to coach. But when the call went out for coaches to assist with the local youth football program, you answered because you like children and enjoy football, and perhaps are interested in starting a coaching career.

I Want to Help, but . . .

Your initial coaching assignment may be difficult. Like many volunteers, you may not know everything there is to know about football, nor about how to work with children between the ages of 7 and 14. Relax, because *Coaching Youth Football* will help you learn the basics for coaching football effectively. In the coming pages you will find the answers to such common questions as these:

- What tools do I need to be a good coach?
- How can I best communicate with my players?
- How do I go about teaching sport skills?
- What can I do to promote safety?
- What should I do when someone is injured?
- What are the basic rules, skills, and strategies of football?
- What practice drills will improve my players' football skills?

Before answering these questions, let's take a look at what's involved in being a coach.

Am I a Parent or a Coach?

Many coaches are parents, but the two roles should not be confused. Unlike your role as a parent, as a coach you are responsible not only to yourself and your child, but also to the organization, all the players on the team (including your child), and their parents. Because of this additional responsibility, your behavior on the football field will be different from your behavior at home, and your son or daughter may not understand why.

For example, imagine the confusion of a young boy who is the center of his parents' attention at home but is barely noticed by his father/coach in the sport setting. Or consider the mixed signals received by a young girl whose football skill is constantly evaluated by a mother/coach who otherwise rarely comments on her daughter's activities. You need to explain to your son or daughter your new responsibilities and how they will affect your relationship when coaching.

Take the following steps to avoid such problems in coaching your child:

- Ask your child if he or she wants you to coach the team.
- Explain why you wish to be involved with the team.
- Discuss with your child how your interactions will change when you take on the role of coach at practices or games.
- Limit your coaching behavior to when you are in the coaching role.
- Avoid parenting during practice or game situations, to keep your role clear in your child's mind.
- Reaffirm your love for your child, irrespective of his or her performance on the football field.

What Are My Responsibilities as a Coach?

A coach assumes the responsibility of doing everything possible to ensure that the youngsters on his or her team will have an enjoyable and safe sporting experience while they learn sport skills. If you're ever in doubt about your approach, remind yourself that "fun and fundamentals" are most important.

Provide an Enjoyable Experience

Football should be fun. Even if nothing else is accomplished, make certain your players have fun. Take the fun out of sport and you'll take the kids out of sport.

Children enter sport for a number of reasons (e.g., to meet and play with other children, to develop physically, and to learn skills), but their major objective is to have fun. Help them satisfy this goal by injecting humor and variety into your practices. Also, make games nonthreatening, festive experiences for your players. Such an approach will increase your players' desire to participate in the future, which should be the biggest goal of youth sport. Unit 2 will help you learn how to satisfy your players' yearning for fun and keep winning in perspective. And unit 3 will describe how you can effectively communicate this perspective to them.

Provide a Safe Experience

You are responsible for planning and teaching activities in such a way that the progression between activities minimizes risks (see units 4 and 5). Further, you must ensure that the field on which your team practices and plays, and the equipment team members use, are free of hazards. Finally, you need to protect yourself from any legal liability issues that might arise from your involvement as a coach. Unit 5 will help you take the appropriate precautions.

Provide Opportunities for Children With Disabilities

There's a possibility that a child with a disability of some kind will register for your team. Don't panic! Your youth sport administrator or a number of organizations (see appendix C) can provide you with information to help you best meet this child's needs.

As a coach, you need to know about the Americans with Disabilities Act (ADA). Passed in 1990, the ADA gives individuals the same legal protection against discrimination on the basis of disabilities as is provided against discrimination on the basis of race, gender, and class. The law does recognize that there are times when including an individual who is disabled might risk the safety of that individual and other players, but the exact way that courts are treating the ADA is still being decided. In general, the law requires that "reasonable accommodations" be made to include children with disabilities into organized sport programs. If a parent or child approaches you on the subject, and you aren't sure what to do, talk to the director in charge of your football program. If you make any decision on your own pertaining to the ADA, you may be vulnerable to a lawsuit.

Keep in mind that these children want to participate alongside their able-bodied peers. Give them the same support and encouragement that you give other athletes, and model their inclusion and acceptance for all your athletes.

Teach Basic Football Skills

In becoming a coach, you take on the role of educator. You must teach your players the fundamental skills and strategies necessary for success in football. That means that you need to "go to school."

If you don't know the basics of football now, you can learn them by reading the second half of this book, units 6, 7, and 8. But even if you know football as a player, do you know how to teach it? This book will help you get started. There are also many valuable football books on the market, including those offered by Human Kinetics. See the list of books in the back of this book or call (800) 747-4457 for more information.

You'll also find it easier to provide good educational experiences for your players if you plan your practices. Unit 4 of this book provides some guidelines for planning effective practices.

Getting Help

Veteran coaches in your league are an especially good source of help for you. These coaches have all experienced the same emotions and concerns you are facing, and their advice and feedback can be invaluable as you work through your first season.

You can also learn a lot by watching local high school and college football coaches in practices and games. You might even ask a few of the coaches you respect most to lend you a hand with a couple of your practices. You can get additional help by attending football clinics, reading football publications, and studying instructional videos. In addition to the American Sport Education Program (ASEP), the following national organizations will assist you in obtaining more football coaching information:

> Pop Warner Football
> 920 Town Center Drive
> Suite I-25
> Langhorne, PA 19047
> (215) 752-2691

> United States Flag and Touch Football League
> 7709 Ohio Street
> Mentor, OH 44060
> (216) 974-8735/phone and fax

Coaching football is a rewarding experience. And, just as you want your players to practice and learn to be the best they can be, you need to learn all you can about coaching in order to be the best football coach you can be.

Unit 2

What Tools Do I Need as a Coach?

Have you purchased the traditional coaching tools—things like footballs, a whistle, a clipboard, and a first aid kit? They'll help you coach, but to be a successful coach you'll need five other tools that cannot be bought. These tools are available only through self-examination and hard work; they're easy to remember using the acronym COACH:

C—Comprehension

O—Outlook

A—Affection

C—Character

H—Humor

Comprehension

Comprehension of the rules, skills, and tactics of football is required. To help you learn about the game, the second half of this book describes how football is played as well as specific techniques and strategies. In the football-specific section of this book, you'll also find a variety of drills to use in developing young players' skills. And, perhaps most important, you'll learn how to apply your knowledge of the game to teach your football team.

To improve your comprehension of football, take the following steps:

- Read the football-specific section of this book.
- Read other football coaching books, including those available from ASEP (see the back of this book for more information).
- Contact Pop Warner Football or United States Flag and Touch Football League (see page 7).
- Attend football coaches' clinics.
- Talk with other, more experienced, football coaches.
- Observe local college, high school, and youth football games.
- Watch televised football games.

In addition to having football knowledge, you must implement proper training and safety methods so your players can participate with little risk of injury. Even then, sport injuries will occur. And more often than not, you'll be the first person responding to your players' injuries, so be sure you understand the basic emergency care procedures described in unit 5. Also, read in that unit how to handle more serious sport injury situations.

Outlook

Outlook refers to your perspective and goals—what you are seeking as a coach. The most common coaching objectives are (a) to have fun, (b) to help players develop their physical, mental, and social

skills, and (c) to win. Thus your outlook involves the priorities you set, your planning, and your vision for the future.

To work successfully with children in a sport setting, you must have your priorities in order. In just what order do you rank the importance of fun, development, and winning?

Answer the following questions to examine your objectives:

Of which situation would you be most proud?
   a. Knowing that each participant enjoyed playing football.
   b. Seeing that all players improved their football skills.
   c. Winning the league championship.

Which statement best reflects your thoughts about sport?
   a. If it isn't fun, don't do it.
   b. Everyone should learn something every day.
   c. Sport isn't fun if you don't win.

How would you like your players to remember you?
   a. As a coach who was fun to play for.
   b. As a coach who provided a good base of fundamental skills.
   c. As a coach who had a winning record.

Which would you most like to hear a parent of a child on your team say?
   a. Billy really had a good time playing football this year.
   b. Susie learned some important lessons playing football this year.
   c. Jose played on the first-place football team this year.

Which of the following would be the most rewarding moment of your season?
   a. Having your team want to continue playing, even after practice is over.
   b. Seeing your players learn how to get off the ball quickly, as a unit, when the ball is snapped.
   c. Winning a game on a play you called.

Look over your answers. If you most often selected "a" responses, then having fun is most important to you. A majority of "b" answers suggests that skill development is what attracts you to coaching. And if "c" was your most frequent response, winning is tops on your list of coaching priorities.

Most coaches say fun and development are more important, but when actually coaching, some coaches emphasize—indeed, overemphasize—winning. You, too, will face situations that challenge you to keep winning in its proper perspective. During such moments, you'll have to choose between emphasizing your players' development or winning. If your priorities are in order, your players' well-being will take precedence over your team's win-loss record every time.

Take the following actions to better define your outlook:

1. Determine your priorities for the season.
2. Prepare for situations that challenge your priorities.
3. Set goals for yourself and your players that are consistent with those priorities.
4. Plan how you and your players can best attain those goals.
5. Review your goals frequently to be sure that you are staying on track.

It is particularly important for coaches to permit all young athletes to participate. Each youngster—male or female, small or tall, gifted or disabled—should have an opportunity to develop skills and have fun.

Remember that the challenge and joy of sport is experienced through striving to win, not through winning itself. Players who aren't allowed off the bench are denied the opportunity to strive to win. And herein lies the irony: Coaches who allow all of their players to participate and develop skills will—in the end—come out on top.

ASEP has a motto that will help you keep your outlook in the best interest of the kids on your team. It summarizes in four words all you need to remember when establishing your coaching priorities:

Athletes First,
Winning Second

This motto recognizes that striving to win is an important, even vital, part of sport. But it emphatically states that no efforts in striving to win should be made at the expense of the athletes' well-being, development, and enjoyment.

Affection

Affection is another vital tool you will want to have in your coaching kit: a genuine concern for the young people you coach. It involves having a love for children, a desire to share with them your love and knowledge of football, and the patience and understanding that allow each individual playing for you to grow from his or her involvement in football.

Successful coaches have a real concern for the health and welfare of their players. They care that each child on the team has an enjoyable and successful experience. They recognize that there are similarities between young people's sport experiences and other activities in their lives, and they encourage their players to strive to learn from all their experiences, to become well-rounded individuals. These coaches have a strong desire to work with children and be involved in their growth. And they have the patience to work with those who are slower to learn or less capable of performing. If you have such qualities or are willing to work hard to develop them, then you have the affection necessary to coach young athletes.

There are many ways to demonstrate your affection and patience, including these:

- Make an effort to get to know each player on your team.
- Treat each player as an individual.

- Empathize with players trying to learn new and difficult football skills.
- Treat players as you would like to be treated under similar circumstances.
- Be in control of your emotions.
- Show your enthusiasm for being involved with your team.
- Keep an upbeat and positive tone in all of your communications.

Some children appreciate a pat on the back or shoulder as a sign of your approval or affection. But be aware that not all players feel comfortable with being touched. When this is the case, you need to respect their wishes.

Character

Character is a word that adults use frequently in conversations about sport experiences and young people. If you haven't already, you may one day be asked to explain whether you think sport builds good character. What will you say?

The fact that you have decided to coach young football players probably means that you think participation in sport is important. But whether or not that participation develops character in your players depends as much on you as it does on the sport itself. How can you build character in your players?

Youngsters learn by listening to what adults say. But they learn even more by watching the behavior of certain important individuals. As a coach, you are likely to be a significant figure in the lives of your players. Will you be a good role model?

Having good character means modeling appropriate behaviors for sport and life. That means more than just saying the right things. What you say and what you do must match. There is no place in coaching for the "Do as I say, not as I do" philosophy. Challenge, support, encourage, and reward every child, and your players will be more likely to accept, even celebrate, their differences. Be in control before, during, and after all games and practices. And don't be afraid to admit that you were wrong. No one is perfect!

Many of us have been coached by someone who believes that criticizing players is a good way to build character. In reality, this approach damages children's self-esteem and teaches them that their value as a person is based on how they perform in sport. Unit 3 will help you communicate with your players in a way that builds positive self-esteem and develops your athletes' skills.

Finally, take stock of your own attitudes about ethnic, gender, and other stereotypes. You are an individual coach, and it would be wrong for others to form beliefs about you based on their personal attitudes about coaches in general. Similarly, you need to avoid making comments that support stereotypes of others. Let your words and actions show your players that every individual matters, and you will be teaching them a valuable lesson about respecting and supporting individuals' differences.

Consider the following steps to being a good role model:

- Take stock of your strengths and weaknesses.
- Build on your strengths.
- Set goals for yourself to improve upon those areas you would not like to see mimicked.
- If you slip up, apologize to your team and to yourself. You'll do better next time.

Humor

Humor is an often-overlooked coaching tool. For our use it means having the ability to laugh at yourself and with your players during practices and games. Nothing helps balance the tone of a serious, skill-learning session like a chuckle or two. And a sense of humor puts in perspective the many mistakes your young players will make. So don't get upset over each miscue or respond negatively to erring players. Allow your players and yourself to enjoy the ups, and don't dwell on the downs.

Here are some tips for injecting humor into your practices:

- Make practices fun by including a variety of activities.
- Keep all players involved in drills and scrimmages.
- Consider laughter by your players a sign of enjoyment, not waning discipline.
- Smile!

Where Do You Stand?

To take stock of your "coaching tool kit," rank yourself on the three questions for each of the five coaching tools. Simply circle the number that best describes your current status on each item.

Not at all		Somewhat		Very much so
1	**2**	**3**	**4**	**5**

Comprehension _____

1. Could you explain the rules of football to other parents without studying for a long time?   1 2 3 4 5

2. Do you know how to organize and conduct safe football practices?   1 2 3 4 5

3. Do you know how to provide first aid for most common, minor sport injuries?   1 2 3 4 5

Comprehension Score: _____

Outlook

4. Do you place the interests of all children ahead of winning when you coach? 1 2 3 4 5

5. Do you plan for every meeting, practice, and game? 1 2 3 4 5

6. Do you have a vision of what you want your players to be able to do by the end of the season? 1 2 3 4 5

Outlook Score: _____

Affection

7. Do you enjoy working with children? 1 2 3 4 5

8. Are you patient with youngsters learning new skills? 1 2 3 4 5

9. Are you able to show your players that you care? 1 2 3 4 5

Affection Score: _____

Character

10. Are your words and behaviors consistent with each other? 1 2 3 4 5

11. Are you a good model for your players? 1 2 3 4 5

12. Do you keep negative emotions under control before, during, and after games? 1 2 3 4 5

Character Score: _____

Humor

13. Do you usually smile at your players? 1 2 3 4 5

14. Are your practices fun? 1 2 3 4 5

15. Are you able to laugh at your mistakes? 1 2 3 4 5

Humor Score: _____

If you scored 9 or less on any of the coaching tools, be sure to reread those sections carefully. And even if you scored 15 on each tool, don't be complacent. Keep learning! Then you'll be well-equipped with the tools you need to coach young athletes.

How Should I Communicate With My Players?

Now you know the tools needed to COACH: Comprehension, Outlook, Affection, Character, and Humor. These are essentials for effective coaching; without them, you'd have a difficult time getting started. But none of those tools will work if you don't know how to use them with your athletes—and this requires skillful communication. This unit examines what communication is and how you can become a more effective communicator-coach.

What's Involved in Communication?

Coaches often mistakenly believe that communication involves only instructing players to do something, but verbal commands are a very small part of the communication process. More than half of what is communicated is nonverbal. So remember when you are coaching: Actions speak louder than words.

Communication in its simplest form is like a quarterback and a receiver. It involves two people: one to pass the message (verbally, through facial expression, and via body language) and the other to receive it. Of course, a receiver who fails to pay attention or judge the message correctly will not catch it.

How Can I Send More Effective Messages?

Young athletes often have little understanding of the rules and skills of football and probably even less confidence in playing it. So they need accurate, understandable, and supportive messages to help them along. That's why your verbal and nonverbal messages are so important.

Verbal Messages

"Sticks and stones may break my bones, but words will never hurt me" isn't true. Spoken words can have a strong and long-lasting effect. And coaches' words are particularly influential because youngsters place great importance on what coaches say. Perhaps you, like many former youth sport participants, have a difficult time remembering much of anything you were told by your elementary school teachers but can still recall several specific things your coaches at that level said to you. Such is the lasting effect of a coach's comments to a player.

Whether you are correcting misbehavior, teaching a player how to tackle, or praising a player for good effort, there are a number of things you should consider when sending a message verbally. They include the following:

- *Be positive and honest.*
- *State it clearly and simply.*
- *Say it loud enough, and say it again.*
- *Be consistent.*

Be Positive and Honest

Nothing turns people off like hearing someone nag all the time, and young athletes react similarly to a coach who gripes constantly. Kids particularly need encouragement because many of them doubt their ability to play football. So look for and tell your players what they did well.

But don't cover up poor or incorrect play with rosy words of praise. Kids know all too well when they've erred, and no cheerfully expressed cliché can undo their mistakes. If you fail to acknowledge players' errors, your athletes will think you are a phony.

State It Clearly and Simply

Positive and honest messages are good, but only if expressed directly in words your players understand. "Beating around the bush" is ineffective and inefficient. And if you do ramble, your players will miss the point of your message and probably lose interest. Here are some tips for saying things clearly:

- Organize your thoughts before speaking to your athletes.
- Explain things thoroughly, but don't bore them with long-winded monologues.

- Use language your players can understand. However, avoid trying to be hip by using their age group's slang vocabulary.

COMPLIMENT SANDWICH

A good way to handle situations in which you have identified and must correct improper technique is to serve your players a "compliment sandwich":

1. Point out what the athlete did correctly.
2. Let the player know what was incorrect in the performance and instruct him or her how to correct it.
3. Encourage the player by reemphasizing what he or she did well.

Say It Loud Enough, and Say It Again

A football field with kids spread out from one end zone to the other can make communication difficult. So talk to your team in a voice that all members can hear and interpret. A crisp, vigorous voice commands attention and respect; garbled and weak speech is tuned out. It's OK, in fact, appropriate, to soften your voice when speaking to a player individually about a personal problem. But most of the time your messages will be for all your players to hear, so make sure they can! An enthusiastic voice also motivates players and tells them you enjoy being their coach. A word of caution, however: Don't dominate the setting with a booming voice that distracts attention from players' performances.

Sometimes what you say, even if stated loud and clear, won't sink in the first time. This may be particularly true with young athletes hearing words they don't understand. To avoid boring repetition and yet still get your message across, say the same thing in a slightly different way. For instance, you might first tell your players "Get an angle on the runner." Soon afterward, remind them "Try to meet and tackle the ballcarrier near or behind the line of scrimmage, without letting him get by you for a touchdown." The second form of the message may get through to players who missed it the first time around.

Be Consistent

People often say things in ways that imply a different message. For example, a touch of sarcasm added to the words "way to go" sends an entirely different message than the words themselves suggest. It is essential that you avoid sending such mixed messages. Keep the tone of your voice consistent with the words you use. And don't say something one day and contradict it the next; players will get confused. If you still aren't certain whether your players understand, ask them to repeat the message back to you. As the old saying goes "If they can't say it, they can't play it."

Nonverbal Messages

Just as you should be consistent in the tone of voice and words you use, you should also keep your verbal and nonverbal messages consistent. An extreme example of failing to do this would be shaking your head, indicating disapproval, while at the same time telling a player "Nice try." Which is the player to believe, your gesture or your words?

Messages can be sent nonverbally in a number of ways. Facial expressions and body language are just two of the more obvious forms of nonverbal signals that can help you when you coach.

Facial Expressions

The look on a person's face is the quickest clue to what he or she thinks or feels. Your players know this, so they will study your face, looking for any sign that will tell them more than the words you say. Don't try to fool them by putting on a happy or blank "mask." They'll see through it, and you'll lose credibility.

Serious, stone-faced expressions are no help to kids who need cues as to how they are performing. They will just assume you're unhappy or disinterested. Don't be afraid to smile. A smile from a coach can give a great boost to an unsure young athlete. Plus, a smile lets your players know that you are happy coaching them. But don't overdo it, or your players won't be able to tell when you are genuinely pleased by something they've done or when you are just putting on a smiling face.

Body Language

What would your players think you were feeling if you came to practice slouched over, with head down and shoulders slumped? Tired? Bored? Unhappy? What would they think you were feeling if you watched them during a game with your hands on your hips, your jaws clenched, and your face reddened? Upset with them? Disgusted at an official? Mad at a fan? Probably some or all of these things would enter your players' minds. And none of these impressions is the kind you want your players to have of you. That's why you should carry yourself in a pleasant, confident, and vigorous manner. Such a posture not only projects happiness with your coaching role but also provides a good example for your young players who may model your behavior.

Physical contact can also be a very important use of body language. A handshake, a pat on the back, an arm around the shoulder, or even a big hug are effective ways of showing approval, concern, affection, and joy to your players. Youngsters are especially in need of this type of nonverbal message. Keep within the obvious moral and legal limits, but don't be reluctant to touch your players and send a message that can only truly be expressed in that way.

How Can I Improve My Receiving Skills?

Now, let's examine the other half of the communication process—receiving messages. Too often people are very good senders but very poor receivers of messages. As a coach of young athletes, it is essential that you are able to fulfill both roles effectively.

The requirements for receiving messages are quite simple, but receiving skills are perhaps less satisfying and therefore underdeveloped compared to sending skills. People seem to naturally enjoy hearing themselves talk more than others. But if you are willing to read about the keys to receiving messages and to make a strong effort to use them with your players, you'll be surprised by what you've been missing.

Attention!

First, you must pay attention; you must want to hear what others have to communicate to you. That's not always easy when you're busy coaching and have many things competing for your attention. But in one-to-one or team meetings with players, you must really focus on what they are telling you, both verbally and nonverbally. You'll be amazed at the little signals you pick up. Not only will such focused attention help you catch every word your players say, but you'll also notice your players' moods and physical states, and you'll get an idea of your players' feelings toward you and other players on the team.

Listen CARE-FULLY

How we receive messages from others, perhaps more than anything else we do, demonstrates how much we care for the sender and what that person has to tell us. If you care little for your players or have little regard for what they have to say, it will show in how you attend and listen to them. Check yourself. Do you find your mind wandering to what you are going to do after practice while one of your players is talking to you? Do you frequently have to ask your players, "What did you say?" If so, you need to work on your receiving mechanics of attending and listening. But perhaps the most critical question you should ask yourself, if you find that you're missing the messages your players send, is this: Do I care?

How Do I Put It All Together?

So far we've discussed separately the sending and receiving of messages. But we all know that senders and receivers switch roles several times during an interaction. One person initiates a communication by sending a message to another person, who then receives the message. The receiver then switches roles and becomes the sender by responding to the person who sent the initial message. These verbal and nonverbal responses are called feedback.

Your players will be looking to you for feedback all the time. They will want to know how you think they are performing, what you think of their ideas, and whether their efforts please you. Obviously, you can respond in many different ways. How you respond will strongly affect your players. So let's take a look at a few general types of feedback and examine their possible effects.

Providing Instructions

With young players, much of your feedback will involve answering questions about how to play football. Your instructive responses to these questions should include both verbal and nonverbal feedback. Here are some suggestions for giving instructional feedback:

- Keep verbal instructions simple and concise.
- Use demonstrations to provide nonverbal instructional feedback (see unit 4).
- "Walk" players through the skill, or use a slow-motion demonstration if they are having trouble learning.

Correcting Errors

When your players perform incorrectly, you need to provide informative feedback to correct the error—and the sooner the better. When you do correct errors, keep in mind these two principles: Use negative criticism sparingly, and keep calm.

Use Negative Criticism Sparingly

Although you may need to punish players for horseplay or dangerous activities by scolding or removing them from activity tempo-

rarily, avoid reprimanding players for performance errors. Admonishing players for honest mistakes makes them afraid to even try. Nothing ruins a youngster's enjoyment of a sport more than a coach who harps on every miscue. So instead, correct your players by using the positive approach. Your players will enjoy playing more, and you'll enjoy coaching more.

Keep Calm

Don't fly off the handle when your players make mistakes. Remember, you're coaching young and inexperienced players, not pros. You'll therefore see more incorrect than correct technique, and you'll probably have more discipline problems than you expect. But throwing a tantrum over each error or misbehavior will only inhibit your players or suggest to them the wrong kind of behavior to model. So let your players know that mistakes aren't the end of the world; stay cool!

Giving Positive Feedback

Praising players when they have performed or behaved well is an effective way of getting them to repeat (or try to repeat) that behavior in the future. And positive feedback for effort is an especially effective way to motivate youngsters to work on difficult skills. So rather than shouting and providing negative feedback to a player who has made a mistake, try offering players a compliment sandwich, described on page 22.

Sometimes just the way you word feedback can make it more positive than negative. For example, instead of saying, "Don't block with your feet like that," you might say, "Block with your feet shoulder-width apart." Then your players will be focusing on what to do instead of what not to do.

Coaches, be positive!

Only a very small percentage of ASEP-trained coaches' behaviors are negative.

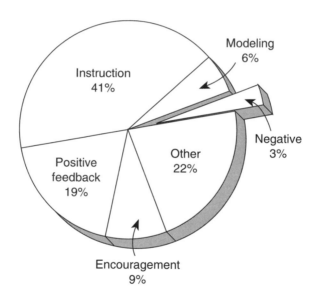

Instruction
41%

Modeling
6%

Negative
3%

Other
22%

Positive
feedback
19%

Encouragement
9%

You can give positive feedback verbally and nonverbally. Telling a player, especially in front of teammates, that he or she has performed well is a great way to boost the youngster's confidence. And a pat on the back or a handshake can be a very tangible way of communicating your recognition of a player's performance.

Who Else Do I Need to Communicate With?

Coaching involves not only sending and receiving messages and providing proper feedback to players, but also interacting with parents, fans, officials, and opposing coaches. If you don't communicate effectively with these groups of people, your coaching career will be unpleasant and short-lived. So try the following suggestions for communicating with these groups.

Parents

A player's parents need to be assured that their son or daughter is under the direction of a coach who is both knowledgeable about football and concerned about the youngster's well-being. You can put their worries to rest by holding a preseason parent orientation meeting in which you describe your background and your approach to coaching.

If parents contact you with a concern during the season, listen to them closely and try to offer positive responses. If you need to communicate with parents, catch them after a practice, give them a phone call, or send a note through the mail. Messages sent to parents through children are too often lost, misinterpreted, or forgotten.

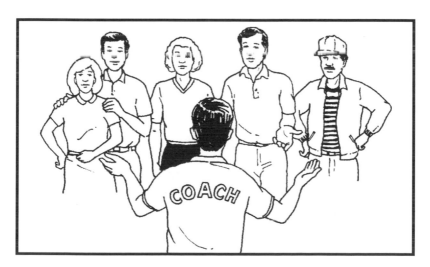

Fans

The stands probably won't be overflowing at your games, but that only means that you'll more easily hear the few fans who criticize your coaching. When you hear something negative said about the job you're doing, don't respond. Keep calm, consider whether the message has any value, and if not, forget it. Acknowledging critical, unwarranted comments from a fan during a game will only encourage others to voice their opinions. So put away your "rabbit ears" and communicate to fans, through your actions, that you are a confident, competent coach.

Even if you are ready to withstand the negative comments of fans, your players may not be. Prepare your players for fans' criticisms. Tell them it is you, not the spectators, to whom they should listen. If you notice that one of your players is rattled by a fan's comment, reassure the player that your evaluation is more objective and favorable—and the one that counts.

Officials

How you communicate with officials will have a great influence on the way your players behave toward them. Therefore, you need to set an example. Greet officials with a handshake, an introduction, and perhaps some casual conversation about the upcoming contest. Indicate your respect for them before, during, and after the game. Don't make nasty remarks, shout, or use disrespectful body gestures. Your players will see you do it, and they'll get the idea that such behavior is appropriate. Plus, if the official hears or sees you, the communication between the two of you will break down.

Opposing Coaches

Make an effort to visit with the coach of the opposing team before the game. Perhaps the two of you can work out a special arrangement for the game, such as matching up players of equal size and strength. During the game, don't get into a personal feud with the opposing coach. Remember, it's the kids, not the coaches, who are competing. And by getting along well with the opposing coach, you'll show your players that competition involves cooperation.

✔ *Summary Checklist*

Now, check your coach-communication skills by answering "Yes" or "No" to the following questions.

	Yes	No
1. Are your verbal messages to your players positive and honest?	___	___
2. Do you speak loudly, clearly, and in a language your athletes understand?	___	___
3. Do you remember to repeat instructions to your players, in case they didn't hear you the first time?	___	___
4. Are the tone of your voice and your nonverbal messages consistent with the words you use?	___	___
5. Do your facial expressions and body language express interest in and happiness with your coaching role?	___	___
6. Are you attentive to your players and able to pick up even their small verbal and nonverbal cues?	___	___
7. Do you really care about what your athletes say to you?	___	___
8. Do you instruct rather than criticize when your players make errors?	___	___
9. Are you usually positive when responding to things your athletes say and do?	___	___
10. Do you try to communicate in a cooperative and respectful manner with players' parents, fans, officials, and opposing coaches?	___	___

If you answered "No" to any of the above questions, you may want to refer back to the section of the chapter where the topic was discussed. Now is the time to address communication problems, not when you're coaching your players.

Unit 4

How Do I Get My Team Ready to Play?

To coach football, you must understand the basic rules, skills, and strategies. The second part of this book provides the basic information you'll need to comprehend the sport.

But all the football knowledge in the world will do you little good unless you present it effectively to your players. That's why this unit is so important. Here you will learn the steps to take when teaching sport skills, as well as practical guidelines for planning your season and individual practices.

How Do I Teach Football Skills?

Many people believe that the only qualification needed to coach is to have played the sport. It's helpful to have played, but there is much more to coaching successfully. Even if you haven't played or even watched football, you can still learn to coach successfully with this IDEA:

I—Introduce the skill.

D—Demonstrate the skill.

E—Explain the skill.

A—Attend to players practicing the skill.

Introduce the Skill

Players, especially young and inexperienced ones, need to know what skill they are learning and why they are learning it. You should therefore take these three steps every time you introduce a skill to your players:

1. Get your players' attention.

2. Name the skill.

3. Explain the importance of the skill.

Get Your Players' Attention

Because youngsters are easily distracted, use some method to get their attention. Some coaches use interesting news items or stories. Others use jokes. And others simply project enthusiasm that gets their players to listen. Whatever method you use, speak slightly above the normal volume and look your players in the eyes when you speak.

Also, position players so they can see and hear you. Arrange the players in two or three evenly spaced rows, facing you and not the sun or some source of distraction. Then ask if everyone can see and hear you before you begin.

Name the Skill

Although you might mention other common names for the skill, decide which one you'll use and stick with it. This will help avoid confusion and enhance communication among your players. For example, choose either "swing pass" or "flare" as the term for the short, quick pass to a back, and use it consistently.

Explain the Importance of the Skill

Although the importance of a skill may be apparent to you, your players may be less able to see how the skill will help them become better football players. Offer them a reason for learning the skill and describe how the skill relates to more advanced skills.

> *"The most difficult aspect of coaching is this: Coaches must learn to let athletes learn. Sport skills should be taught so they have meaning to the child, not just meaning to the coach."*
>
> Rainer Martens, ASEP Founder

Demonstrate the Skill

The demonstration step is the most important part of teaching a football skill to young players who may have never done anything closely resembling it. They need a picture, not just words. They need to see how the skill is performed.

If you are unable to perform the skill correctly, have an assistant coach or someone skilled in football perform the demonstration. A high school varsity player would be an excellent choice. These tips will help make your demonstrations more effective:

- Use correct form.
- Demonstrate the skill several times.
- Slow down the skill, if possible, during one or two performances so players can see every movement involved.
- Perform the skill at different angles so your players can get a full perspective of it.
- Demonstrate the skill from both the right and left sides.

Explain the Skill

Players learn more effectively when they're given a brief explanation of the skill along with the demonstration. Use simple terms to describe the skill and, if possible, relate it to previously learned skills. Ask your players whether they understand your description. A good technique is to ask the team to repeat your explanation. Ask questions like "What are you going to do first?" "Then what?" Watch for looks of confusion or uncertainty and repeat your explanation and demonstration of those points. If possible, use different words so that your players get a chance to try to understand from a different perspective.

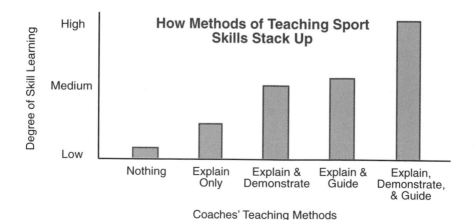

Coaches' Teaching Methods

Complex skills often are better understood when they are explained in more manageable parts. For instance, if you want to teach your players how to tackle a ballcarrier when a blocker is coming at them, you might take the following steps:

1. Show them a correct performance of the entire skill and explain its function in football.
2. Break down the skill and point out its component parts to your players.
3. Have players perform each of the component skills you have already taught them, such as getting in their stance, firing off the ball, identifying where the play is going and who has the ball, fending off the blocker, pursuing the ballcarrier, and making the tackle.
4. After players have demonstrated their ability to perform the separate parts of the skill in sequence, reexplain the entire skill.
5. Have players practice the skill.

One caution: Young players have short attention spans, and a long demonstration or explanation of the skill will bore them. So spend no more than a few minutes combined on the introduction, demonstration, and explanation phases. Then get the players active in attempts to perform the skill. The total IDEA should be completed in 10 minutes or less, followed by individual and group practice activities.

Attend to Players Practicing the Skill

If the skill you selected was within your players' capabilities, and you have done an effective job of introducing, demonstrating, and explaining it, your players should be ready to attempt the skill. Some players may need to be physically guided through the movements during their first few attempts. For example, some players may need your hands-on help to get their feet in the correct position for their three-point stance. Walking unsure athletes through the skill in this way will help them gain confidence to perform the skill on their own.

Your teaching duties don't end when all your athletes have demonstrated that they understand how to perform the skill. In fact, a significant part of your teaching will involve observing closely the hit-and-miss trial performances of your players.

As you observe players' efforts in drills and activities, offer positive, corrective feedback in the form of the compliment sandwich described in unit 3. If a player performs the skill properly, acknowledge it and offer praise. Keep in mind that your feedback will have a great influence on your players' motivation to practice and improve their performance.

Remember, too, that young players need individual instruction. So set aside a time before, during, or after practice to give individual help.

What Planning Do I Need to Do?

Beginning coaches often make the mistake of showing up for the first practice with no particular plan in mind. These coaches find that their practices are unorganized, their players are frustrated and inattentive, and the amount and quality of their skill instruction is limited. Planning is essential to successful teaching and coaching. And it doesn't begin on the way to practice!

Preseason Planning

Effective coaches begin planning well before the start of the season. Among the preseason measures that will make the season more enjoyable, successful, and safe for you and your players are the following:

- Familiarize yourself with the sport organization you are involved in, especially its philosophy and goals regarding youth sport.
- Examine the availability of facilities, equipment, instructional aids, and other materials needed for practices and games.
- Find out what fund-raising you and your players will be expected to do, and decide on the best way to meet your goals.
- Make arrangements for any team travel that will be required during the season. Consider clearance forms, supervision, transportation, equipment, contacting parents, and safety.
- Check to see whether you have adequate liability insurance to cover you if one of your players gets hurt (see unit 5). If you don't, get some.
- Establish your coaching priorities regarding having fun, developing players' skills, and winning.
- Select and meet with your assistant coaches to discuss the philosophy, goals, team rules, and plans for the season.
- Register players for the team. Have them complete a player information form and obtain medical clearance forms, if required.
- Institute an injury-prevention program for your players.
- Hold an orientation meeting to inform parents of your background, philosophy, goals, and instructional approach. Also, give a brief overview of the league's rules, terms, and strategies to familiarize parents or guardians with the sport.

You may be surprised at the number of things you should do even before the first practice. But if you address them during the preseason, the season will be much more enjoyable and productive for you and your players.

In-Season Planning

Your choice of activities during the season should be based on whether they will help your players develop physical and mental skills, knowledge of rules and game tactics, sportsmanship, and love for the sport. All of these goals are important, but we'll focus on the skills and tactics of football to give you an idea of how to itemize your objectives.

Goal Setting

What you plan to do during the season must be reasonable for the maturity and skill level of your players. In terms of football skills and tactics, you should teach young players the basics and move on to more complex activities only after the players have mastered these easier techniques and strategies.

To begin the season, your instructional goals might include the following:

- Players will be able to get into a correct stance for any position they might play.
- Players will be able to use proper footwork for the positions they play.
- Players will be able to demonstrate correct positioning for effective blocking.
- Players will be able to demonstrate proper and safe tackling techniques.
- Players will be able to demonstrate knowledge of the rules of football.
- Players will be able to line up in the correct position on offense and defense.
- Players will be able to demonstrate teamwork throughout the season.
- Players will be able to demonstrate their preparation for practices and games during those events.

- Players will be able to demonstrate a basic understanding of offensive and defensive strategies.
- Players will be able to demonstrate good sportsmanship at all times.
- Players will increase their enjoyment of football and develop an interest in learning more about the game.

Organizing

After you've defined the skills and tactics you want your players to learn during the season, you can plan how to teach them to your players in practices. But be flexible! If your players are having difficulty learning a skill or tactic, take some extra time until they get the hang of it—even if that means moving back your schedule. After all, if your players are unable to perform the fundamental skills, they'll never execute the more complex skills you have scheduled for them, and they won't have much fun trying.

Still, it helps to have a plan for progressing players through skills during the season. The sample 12-session plan in appendix A shows how to schedule your skill instruction in an organized and progressive manner. If this is your first coaching experience, you may wish to follow the plan as it stands. If you have some previous experience, you may want to modify the schedule to better fit the needs of your team.

The way you organize your season may also help your players to develop socially and psychologically. By giving your players responsibility for certain aspects of practices—leading warm-up and stretching activities are common examples—you help players to develop self-esteem and take responsibility for themselves and the team. As you plan your season, consider ways to provide your players with experiences that lead them to steadily improve these skills.

What Makes Up a Good Practice?

A good instructional plan makes practice preparation much easier. Have players work on more important and less difficult goals in early-season practice sessions. And see to it that players master basic skills before moving on to more advanced ones.

It is helpful to establish one goal for each practice, but try to include a variety of activities related to that goal. For example, although your primary objective might be to improve players' tackling ability, you should have players perform several different drills designed to enhance that single skill. To add more variety to your practices, vary the order of the activities you schedule for players to perform.

In general, we recommend that in each of your practices you do the following:

- *Warm up.*
- *Practice previously taught skills.*
- *Teach and practice new skills.*
- *Practice under competitive conditions.*
- *Cool down.*
- *Evaluate.*

Warm Up

As you're checking the roster and announcing the performance goals for the practice, your players should be preparing their bodies for vigorous activity. A 5- to 10-minute period of easy-paced activities (three-quarter-speed running around the field), stretching, and calisthenics should be sufficient for youngsters to limber their muscles and reduce the risk of injury.

Practice Previously Taught Skills

Devote part of each practice to having players work on the fundamental skills they already know. But remember, kids like variety.
Thus you should organize and modify drills so that everyone is involved and stays interested. Praise and encourage players when you
notice improvement, and offer individual assistance to those who
need help.

Teach and Practice New Skills

Gradually build on your players' existing skills by giving players
something new to practice each session. The proper method for teaching sport skills is described on pages 36–40. Refer to those pages if
you have any questions about teaching new skills or if you want to
evaluate your teaching approach periodically during the season.

Practice Under Competitive Conditions

Competition among teammates during practices prepares players
for actual games and informs young athletes about their abilities
relative to their peers. Youngsters also seem to have more fun in
competitive activities.

You can create game-like conditions by using competitive drills, modified games, and scrimmages (see units 7 and 8). However, consider the following guidelines before introducing competition into your practices:

- All players should have an equal opportunity to participate.
- Match players by ability and physical maturity.
- Make sure that players can execute fundamental skills before they compete in groups.
- Emphasize performing well, not winning, in every competition.
- Give players room to make mistakes by avoiding constant evaluation of their performances.

Cool Down

Each practice should wind down with a 5- to 10-minute period of light exercise, including jogging, performance of simple skills, and some stretching. The cool-down allows athletes' bodies to return to the resting state and avoid stiffness, and it affords you an opportunity to review the practice.

Evaluate

At the end of practice spend a few minutes with your players reviewing how well the session accomplished the goals you had set. Even if your evaluation is negative, show optimism for future practices and send players off on an upbeat note.

How Do I Put a Practice Together?

Simply knowing the six practice components is not enough. You must also be able to arrange those components into a logical progression and fit them into a time schedule. Now, using your instructional goals as a guide for selecting what skills to have your players work on, try to plan several football practices you might conduct. The following examples should help you get started.

Sample Practice Plan—Tackle Football

Performance Objective. Players will be able to use proper tackling techniques.

Component	Time	Activity or drill
Warm up	10 min	Easy running Stretching Pick-ups
Practice previously taught skills	25 min	Defensive positioning Blocking Fending off blockers
Teach and practice new skills	15 min	Head-on tackling Angle tackling Open-field tackling
Practice under competitive conditions	20 min	Form Tackling Drill Sideline Tackling Drill Small-sided scrimmage
Cool down and evaluate	10 min	3/4-speed offensive plays Stretching Coach's comments

Sample Practice Plan—Flag and Touch Football

Performance Objective. Players will be able to use proper flag pulling and/or touching techniques.

Component	Time	Activity or drill
Warm up	10 min	Easy running Stretching Calisthenics
Practice previously taught skills	25 min	Defensive positioning Noncontact screen blocking Contact blocking Avoiding blocks
Teach and practice new skills	15 min	Head-on flag pulling or touching Angle flag pulling or touching Open-field flag pulling or touching

(continued)

Practice under competitive conditions	20 min	Form Flag Pulling and Touching Drill
		Sideline Flag Pulling Drill or
		  Sideline Touching Drill
		Team scrimmage—offense vs.
		  defense (Separate teams for
		  even number per side if not able
		  to have a full team scrimmage.)

Cool down and evaluate	10 min	3/4-speed offensive plays
		3/4-speed defensive
		  alignments and plays
		3/4-speed special team
		  alignments and plays
		Short jog
		Stretching
		Coach's comments

✔ Summary Checklist

During your football season, check your planning and teaching skills periodically. As you gain more coaching experience, you should be able to answer "Yes" to each of the following.

When you plan, do you remember to plan for

____ preseason events such as player registration, fund-raising, travel, liability protection, use of facilities, and parent orientation?

____ season goals such as the development of players' physical skills, mental skills, sportsmanship, and enjoyment?

____ practice components such as warm-up, practicing previously taught skills, teaching and practicing new skills, practicing under competitive conditions, cool-down, and evaluation?

When you teach football skills to your players, do you

____ arrange the players so all can see and hear?

____ introduce the skill clearly and explain its importance?

____ demonstrate the skill properly several times?

____ explain the skill simply and accurately?

____ attend closely to players practicing the skill?

____ offer corrective, positive feedback or praise after observing players' attempts at the skill?

Unit 5

What About Safety?

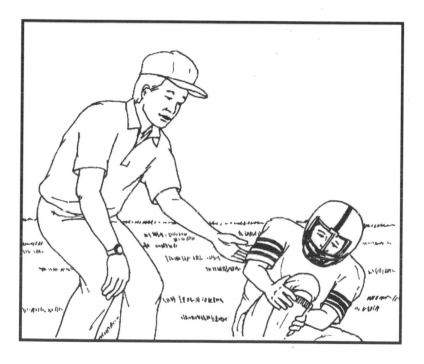

Your fullback breaks free through a huge hole in the line, and it appears he has daylight all the way to the end zone. Suddenly, a linebacker comes from nowhere and makes a crushing tackle on the runner. Although momentarily pleased with the yardage gained on the play, you quickly become concerned when you see that the ballcarrier is not able to get back on his feet. He seems to be in pain. What do you do?

No coach wants to see players get hurt. But injury remains a reality of sport participation; consequently, you must be prepared to provide first aid when injuries occur and to protect yourself against unjustified lawsuits. Fortunately, there are many preventive measures coaches can institute to reduce the risk. This unit will describe how you can

- create the safest possible environment for your players,
- provide emergency first aid to players when they get hurt, and
- protect yourself from injury liability.

How Do I Keep My Players From Getting Hurt?

Injuries may occur because of poor preventive measures. Part of your planning, described in unit 4, should include steps that give your players the best possible chance for injury-free participation. These steps include the following:

- *Preseason physical examination*
- *Nutrition*
- *Physical conditioning*
- *Equipment and facilities inspection*
- *Matching athletes by physical maturity and warning of inherent risks*
- *Proper supervision and record keeping*
- *Providing water breaks*
- *Warm-up and cool-down*

Preseason Physical Examination

In the absence of severe injury or ongoing illness, your players should have a physical examination every 2 years. If a player has a known complication, a physician's consent should be obtained before participation is allowed. You should also have players' parents or guardians sign a participation agreement form and a release form to allow their children to be treated in case of an emergency.

INFORMED CONSENT FORM

I hereby give my permission for _____ to participate

in _____ during the athletic season beginning in 199____.
Further, I authorize the school to provide emergency treatment of an injury to or illness of my child if qualified medical personnel consider treatment necessary *and* perform the treatment. This authorization is granted only if I cannot be reached and a reasonable effort has been made to do so.

Date _____   Parent or guardian _____

Address _____   Phone ( ) _____

Family physician _____   Phone ( ) _____

Pre-existing medical conditions (e.g., allergies or chronic illnesses) _____
_____

Other(s) to also contact in case of emergency _____

Relationship to child _____   Phone ( ) _____

My child and I are aware that participating in _____
is a potentially hazardous activity. I assume all risks associated with participation in this sport, including but not limited to falls, contact with other participants, the effects of the weather, traffic, and other reasonable risk conditions associated with the sport. All such risks to my child are known and understood by me.

I understand this informed consent form and agree to its conditions on behalf of my child.

Child's signature _____   Date _____

Parent's signature _____   Date _____

Nutrition

Increasingly, disordered eating and unhealthy dietary habits are affecting youth football players. Let players and parents know the importance of healthy eating and the dangers that can arise from efforts to lose weight too quickly. Young football players need to supply their bodies with the extra energy they need to keep up with the demands of practices and games. Ask your director about information that you can pass on to your players and their parents, and include a discussion of basic, commonsense nutrition in your parent orientation meeting.

Physical Conditioning

Muscles, tendons, and ligaments unaccustomed to vigorous and long-lasting physical activity are prone to injury. Therefore, prepare your athletes to withstand the exertion of playing football. An effective conditioning program for football would involve running sprints and strength training.

Make conditioning drills and activities fun. Include a skill component, such as firing out of a stance, to prevent players from becoming bored or looking upon the activity as work. A flag pulling or touching drill would be a good drill to add for young players to develop their flag and touch football skills and make the practices fun and exciting.

Keep in mind, too, that players on your team may respond differently to conditioning activities. Wide-ranging levels of fitness or natural ability might mean that an activity that challenges one child is beyond another's ability to complete safely. The environment is another factor that may affect players' responses to activity. The same workout that was effective on a cool morning might be hazardous to players on a hot, humid afternoon. Similarly, an activity children excel in at sea level might present a risk at higher altitudes. An ideal conditioning program prepares players for the season's demands without neglecting physical and environmental factors that affect their safety.

Equipment and Facilities Inspection

Another way to prevent injuries is to check the quality and fit of the clothes and protective equipment used by your players. Slick-soled, poor fitting, or unlaced football shoes are a knee or ankle injury waiting to happen. Make sure your players' shoes have the appropriate-sized studs, are the proper size for their feet, and are double-tied to prevent self-inflicted "shoestring tackles." Two pairs of socks are better than one for preventing blisters.

The pants, pads, jerseys, and helmets your players wear will probably be supplied by your local youth sport program. Check the quality of all equipment and uniforms before fitting them to the kids on your team. After distributing good, proper-fitting equipment, show players how to put on every part of their uniforms. Advise them to wear an undershirt beneath their shoulder pads to reduce the chance of skin irritations.

Make certain that each player on the field has a mouthpiece in place at all times. And tell your athletes that the only time their chin straps should be unsnapped is when they are on the sidelines.

For flag and touch football, check the quality of the flags worn by your players to ensure their safety (especially the safety of their hands when pulling a flag).

Remember, also, to examine regularly the field on which your players practice and play. Remove hazards, report conditions you cannot remedy, and request maintenance as necessary. If unsafe conditions exist, either make adaptations to avoid risk to your players' safety or stop the practice or game until safe conditions have been restored.

Matching Athletes by Physical Maturity and Warning of Inherent Risks

Children of the same age may differ in height and weight by up to 6 inches and 50 pounds. In football, the advantage of size and maturity is critical. It is not fair or safe to pit an underdeveloped young athlete against a player whose physique belongs in the NFL. Try to give smaller, less mature children a better chance to succeed and avoid injury, and larger children more of a challenge. Experience, ability, and emotional maturity are additional factors to keep in mind when matching players on the field.

Matching helps protect you from certain liability concerns. But you also must warn players of the inherent risks involved in playing football, because "failure to warn" is one of the most successful arguments in lawsuits against coaches. So, thoroughly explain the inherent risks of football, and make sure each player knows, understands, and appreciates those risks.

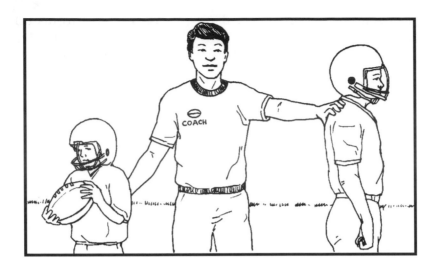

The preseason parent orientation meeting is a good opportunity to explain the risks of football to parents and players. It is also a good occasion on which to have both the players and their parents sign waivers releasing you from liability should an injury occur. Such waivers do not relieve you of responsibility for your players' well-being, but they are recommended by lawyers.

Proper Supervision and Record Keeping

When you work with youngsters, your mere presence in the area of play is not enough; you must actively plan and direct team activities and closely observe and evaluate players' participation. You're the watchdog responsible for the players' well-being. So if you notice a player limping or grimacing, give him or her a rest and examine the extent of the injury.

As a coach, you're also required to enforce the rules of the sport, prohibit dangerous horseplay, and hold practices and games only under safe weather conditions. These specific supervisory activities will make the play environment safer for your players and will help protect you from liability if a mishap does occur.

For further protection, keep records of your season plans, practice plans, and players' injuries. Season and practice plans come in handy when you need evidence that players have been taught certain skills, whereas accurate, detailed accident report forms offer protection against unfounded lawsuits. Ask for these forms from the organization to which you belong. And hold onto these records for several years so that an "old football injury" of a former player doesn't come back to haunt you.

Providing Water Breaks

Tackle, flag, and touch football are extremely vigorous aerobic activities. You know how hot and humid it can get out on a football field when you're wearing a helmet and all that padding. And if you add to that a lot of activity and competition, body temperatures can really rise. Encourage players to drink plenty of water before, during, and after practices and games. Because water makes up 45% to 65% of a youngster's body weight and water weighs about a pound per pint, the loss of even a little water can have severe consequences for the body's systems. And it doesn't have to be hot and humid for players to become dehydrated. Nor do players have to feel thirsty; in fact, by the time they are aware of their thirst, they are long overdue for a drink.

Warm-Up and Cool-Down

Although young bodies are generally very limber, they, too, can get tight from inactivity. Therefore, a warm-up period of approximately 10 minutes before each practice is strongly recommended. The warm-up should address each muscle group and get the heart rate elevated in preparation for strenuous activity. Easy running and stretching, followed by more vigorous calisthenics like jumping jacks, sit-ups, and push-ups, is a common sequence.

As practice is winding down, slow players' heart rates with some moderate then easy-paced activities. Continuous, half-speed execution of all your running plays can be a good way to cool down and review simultaneously. Before you call it a day, arrange for a 5- to 10-minute period of easy stretching at the end of practice to help players avoid stiff muscles and make them less tight before the next practice.

What if One of My Players Gets Hurt?

No matter how good and thorough your prevention program, injuries will occur. When injury does strike, chances are you will be the one in charge. The severity and nature of the injury will determine how actively involved you'll be in treating the injury. But regardless of how seriously a player is hurt, it is your responsibility to know what steps to take. So let's look at how you can provide basic emergency care to your injured athletes.

ASEP Fact

The reported injury rate for youth tackle football is approximately 15%.

Minor Injuries

Although no injury seems minor to the person experiencing it, most injuries are neither life threatening nor severe enough to restrict participation. When such injuries occur, you can take an active role in their initial treatment.

ASEP Fact

You shouldn't let a fear of acquired immune deficiency syndrome (AIDS) stop you from helping a player. On the field you are only at risk if you allow contaminated blood to come in contact with an open wound, so the blood barrier that you wear will protect you from AIDS should one of your players carry this disease. Check with your director or ASEP for more information about protecting yourself and your participants from AIDS.

Scrapes and Cuts

When one of your players has an open wound, the first thing you should do is to put on a pair of disposable surgical gloves or some other effective blood barrier. Then follow these four steps:

1. <u>Stop the bleeding</u> by applying direct pressure with a clean dressing to the wound and elevating it. The player may be able to apply this pressure while you put on your gloves. Do not remove the dressing if it becomes soaked with blood. Instead, place an additional dressing on top of the one already in place. If bleeding continues, elevate the injured area above the heart and maintain pressure.

2. <u>Cleanse the wound</u> thoroughly once the bleeding is controlled. A good rinsing with a forceful stream of water, and perhaps light scrubbing with soap, will help prevent infection.

3. <u>Protect the wound</u> with sterile gauze or a bandage. If the player continues to participate, apply protective padding over the injured area.

4. <u>Remove and dispose of gloves</u> carefully to prevent you or anyone else from coming into contact with blood.

For bloody noses not associated with serious facial injury, have the athlete sit and lean slightly forward. Then pinch the player's nostrils shut. If the bleeding continues after several minutes, or if the athlete has a history of nosebleeds, seek medical assistance.

Strains and Sprains

The physical demands of football practices and games often result in injury to the muscles or tendons (strains), or to the ligaments (sprains). When your players suffer minor strains or sprains, immediately apply the PRICE method of injury care (see page 58).

ASEP Fact

The area most frequently injured by children participating in youth football is the upper body. Fractures, sprains, bruises, and strains are the most common problems.

Bumps and Bruises

Inevitably, football players make contact with each other and with the ground. If the force of a body part at impact is great enough, a bump or bruise will result. Many players continue playing with such sore spots, but if the bump or bruise is large and painful, you should

The PRICE Method

P—Protect the athlete and injured body part from further danger or further trauma.

R—Rest the area to avoid further damage and foster healing.

I —Ice the area to reduce swelling and pain.

C—Compress the area by securing an ice bag in place with an elastic wrap.

E—Elevate the injury above heart level to keep the blood from pooling in the area.

act appropriately. Enact the PRICE method for injury care and monitor the injury. If swelling, discoloration, and pain have lessened, the player may resume participation with protective padding; if not, the player should be examined by a physician.

Serious Injuries

Head, neck, and back injuries; fractures; and injuries that cause a player to lose consciousness are among a class of injuries that you cannot, and should not, try to treat yourself. But you should plan for what you'll do if such an injury occurs. Your plan should include the following guidelines for action:

- Obtain the phone number and ensure the availability of nearby emergency care units. Include this information as part of a written emergency plan before the season, and have it with you at every practice and game.

- Assign an assistant coach or another adult the responsibility of knowing the location of the nearest phone and contacting emergency medical help upon your request.
- Ensure that emergency medical information, treatment, and transportation consent forms are available during every practice and game.
- Do not move the injured athlete.
- Calm the injured athlete and keep others away from him or her as much as possible.
- Evaluate whether the athlete's breathing is stopped or irregular, and if necessary, clear the airway with your fingers.
- Administer artificial respiration if breathing is stopped. Administer cardiopulmonary resuscitation (CPR), or have a trained individual administer CPR if the athlete's circulation has stopped.
- Remain with the athlete until medical personnel arrive.

How Do I Protect Myself?

When one of your players is injured, naturally your first concern is his or her well-being. Your feelings for children, after all, are what made you decide to coach. Unfortunately, there is something else that you must consider: Can you be held liable for the injury?

From a legal standpoint, a coach has nine duties to fulfill. We've discussed all but planning (see unit 4) in this unit:

1. Provide a safe environment.

2. Properly plan the activity.

3. Provide adequate and proper equipment.

4. Match or equate athletes.

5. Warn of inherent risks in the sport.

6. Supervise the activity closely.

7. Evaluate athletes for injury or incapacitation.

8. Know emergency procedures and first aid.

9. Keep adequate records.

In addition to fulfilling these nine legal duties, you should check your insurance coverage to make sure your policy will protect you from liability.

Summary Self-Test

Now that you've read how to make your coaching experience safe for your players and yourself, test your knowledge of the material by answering these questions:

1. What are eight injury-prevention measures you can institute to try to keep your players from getting hurt?
2. What is the four-step emergency care process for cuts?
3. What method of treatment is best for minor sprains and strains?
4. What steps can you take to manage serious injuries?
5. What are the nine legal duties of a coach?

Unit 6

What Is Football All About?

Football is perhaps the most popular sport in the United States. Television ratings for National Football League games are higher than for any other sporting event. At the college level, many football teams draw more than 50,000 fans to each game. And hundreds of thousands of high school athletes practice and work out year-round, making interscholastic football more competitive, specialized, and sophisticated than ever before.

The scene is somewhat different in organized youth football, though the sport means just as much to the participants. Youth football gives many kids their first experience with uniforms, rules and officials to enforce them, striped and marked fields of play, and spectators. An even bigger change from their neighborhood pickup games is that they now have someone coaching them—you!

Coaching Youth Football

Because of football's popularity in this country, you probably watched or played the sport for several years before you became a coach. What you learned in any previous spectating, playing, and coaching experiences will help. But it does not ensure that you will be an effective youth football coach.

In many ways, coaching a youth football team is more difficult than coaching in the NFL. Among your biggest challenges are helping your players

- learn the game,
- participate safely, and
- have as much fun as they would if you weren't around.

This unit, as well as units 7 and 8, will help you face these challenges. Read, learn, and use the information so you can be the kind of coach your players want and deserve.

Approaches to Football

Tackle football and flag and touch football differ in several respects. In the game of tackle football, the object is to stop the forward progress of the ballcarrier by a tackle that forces the ballcarrier to the ground. In the game of flag football, the object is to stop the forward progress of the ballcarrier by pulling his flag. In the game of touch football, the object is to stop the forward progress of the ballcarrier by touching or tagging him with two hands. Because flag and touch football do not allow as much physical contact as tackle football, they provide a much safer way to play the game. The rules prohibit equipment such as helmets and shoulder pads, so flag or touch football is much less expensive. In flag and touch football, ability depends more on age than it does on size. Because the rules permit only limited contact, a small child may play a large child on even terms. This situation cannot take place on a tackle football field! Starting at 6 years of age, the preferred age requirements for flag and touch football are as follows: 6 and under, 8 and under, 10 and under, 12 and under, 14 and under, 16 and under, and 18 and under. Flag and touch football have all the exciting elements of tackle football—the strategies, long runs, scoring, broken plays, and so forth—without the fear of injury.

Field of Play

You probably won't have much to say about the field where your team practices and plays. It is your duty, however, to inspect the field before each practice session and game. If you spot any problems, correct those you can, and ask league administrators to correct those you cannot remedy.

Your field won't look much like the manicured, professionally chalked and painted carpets you see in televised games. And don't be surprised if it also looks a little smaller than usual. Most youth programs follow Pop Warner Football's guidelines for fields, with 80 yards between goal lines and 40 yards between sidelines (see figure 6.1). Some programs start players on even smaller 60-by-30-yard fields.

In flag and touch football, your field is broken into stationary 20-yard zones with first downs being achieved by crossing the next *zone line to gain* (see figure 6.2). For example, it can be first down and 2 yards to go or first down and 19 yards to go, with the first down reached at the next zone line to gain! Field dimensions can be altered to fit your needs or constraints of space (see figure 6.3, a-b).

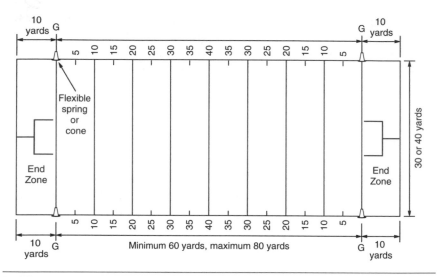

■ **Figure 6.1** Regulation tackle football field.

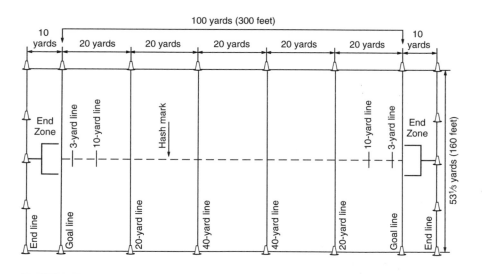

■ **Figure 6.2** Regulation touch and flag football field.

Ball

Just as the size of the field is reduced to match players' development, so too is the size of the ball (see tables 6.1 and 6.2). Your league will probably distribute to all teams a certain size and brand of ball

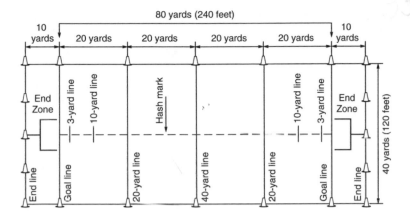

a.

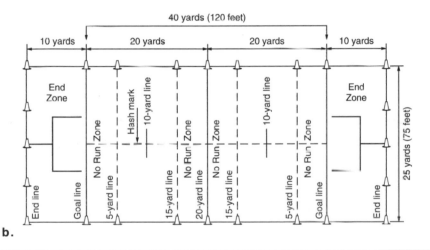

b.

■ **Figure 6.3** (a) Abbreviated touch and flag football field and (b) four-on-four touch and flag football field.

to use throughout the season. The ball will have a set of laces and a leather, rubber, or plastic surface. Check the air pressure of the inflated rubber bladder inside to make sure it agrees with the pressure amount designated on the ball's exterior.

Any junior or youth size ball is allowed. The smaller size lets a younger player learn the proper techniques of throwing or carrying a football at an earlier age.

Table 6.1
Pop Warner Football Designated
Age-Group Divisions and Ball Dimensions

Age Group	Division	Football Dimensions (inches)
7-9	Mighty Mites	10-1/4 to 10 1/2
8-10	Junior Pee Wees	
9-11	Pee Wees	
10-12	Junior Midgets	10-5/8 to 10-3/4
11-13	Midgets	
12-14	Junior Bantams	
14	Bantams	11 to 11-1/2 (regulation)

Table 6.2
USFTL Designated
Age-Group Divisions and Ball Dimensions

Age Group	Football Dimensions
6 and under	In flag and touch football, the quarterback may choose the size of ball he will use. If he has a large hand, he may choose to use a regulation-size ball. If he has a small hand, he may use a smaller ball (youth, junior, or intermediate).
8 and under	
10 and under	
12 and under	
14 and under	
16 and under	
18 and under	

Protective Equipment and Uniform

The physical nature of tackle football requires that players wear protective gear. These items include the helmet, mouthguard, shoulder pads, girdle pads, thigh pads, knee pads, and shoes.

Examine the condition of each item you distribute to players. Also check that the pieces of equipment they furnish for themselves meet acceptable standards.

In addition, it is important that each piece of equipment is fit to the player. Check that each athlete on your team is outfitted properly. That means following the guidelines in figure 6.4 for fitting a tackle football uniform to a player and in figure 6.5 for fitting a flag or touch football uniform to a player.

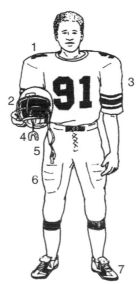

■ **Figure 6.4** Tackle football equipment:
1. *Shoulder pads.* Body padding should not extend beyond tip of shoulder; neck area should fit snugly when arms are extended over head.
2. *Helmet.* Must fit snugly around head and in jaw section; head should be in contact with crown suspension when front edge is approximately one inch above the eyebrow.
3. *Clothing.* Jersey should fit close to body and should always be tucked in pants to hold shoulder pad in place; pants should hug body to keep thigh and knee guards in place.
4. *Mouthguard.*
5. *Girdle pads.* Hip pads must cover point of hip and give proper lower-spine protection.
6. *Thigh and knee pads.* Must be the proper size and inserted properly into the lining of player's pants.
7. *Shoes.* Cleats should be inspected regularly to ensure even wear and stability; proper width is very important; upper should never "overrun" outsole.

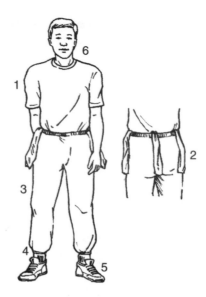

■ **Figure 6.5** Touch and flag football equipment:
1. *T-shirt or jersey.* Should be tucked in so hands are not injured reaching for flags.
2. *Flags.* Flag football only.
3. *Shorts, football pants, or sweatpants.*
4. *Socks.*
5. *Shoes.* Tennis shoes or spikes with plastic cleats only.
6. *Mouthguard.*

You may have to demonstrate to players how to put on each piece of equipment. Otherwise, expect some of them to show up for the first practice with their shoulder pads on backward and their thigh pads upside down.

Shaping a mouthguard is also a mystery to most youngsters. Although these plastic mouthpieces come with easy-to-follow directions, your players may need further guidance. Take some time to explain the heating and shaping process. Just being on a real football field will give some young players lumps in their throats; they don't need to be choking on a cumbersome mouthguard at the same time.

The helmet is the most commonly misused piece of football equipment. So before distributing helmets to your players, explain very clearly that a helmet is a protective covering, not a weapon. If you spot a player using the helmet as a battering device, take him aside and demonstrate the correct, heads-up technique.

How the Game Is Played

The game begins with a kickoff. A player on one team kicks the ball from a designated yard line off a tee toward the opponent's goal line. A player on either team can field the ball after it travels 10 yards downfield. If, as usually happens, a player on the receiving team gains possession, that player tries to advance the ball as far as possible toward the kicking team's goal line. The kicking team tries to tackle the ballcarrier, pull the ballcarrier's flag (in flag football), or touch the ballcarrier (in touch football), as close to the receiving team's goal as possible. When any of these three things happen or the ballcarrier runs out of bounds, the officials whistle the ball dead and momentarily stop play.

The point where play resumes is called the *line of scrimmage*. The line of scrimmage stretches from one sideline to the other, passing through the point of the ball nearest the defense. The team with the ball is the offense; the opposing team is the defense. In 11-man football, the offensive team must begin each play with at least 7 players lined up on the line of scrimmage, facing the defense. Each play starts when one of these linemen, the center, snaps the ball to a teammate, typically the quarterback.

The offense is allowed four plays, or *downs*, to advance the football 10 yards toward the opponent's goal line. If successful, the offense is given a new set of downs and can maintain possession until it

- is stopped by the defense and has to *punt*, typically on fourth down;
- turns the ball over to the defense by means of a *fumble*, *interception*, or failure to gain 10 yards in four attempts;
- attempts a *field goal;* or
- scores a *touchdown*.

In flag and touch football, a team achieves a first down by passing a stationary *zone line to gain*, located at the 20- and 40-yard lines.

Team Objectives

The primary objective of the offensive team is to score, although many coaches also want their offense to maintain possession of the ball for as long as possible. By doing so, they reduce the number of chances that the opposing team's offense has to score (see "What's the Score?").

The defensive team's main objective is to prevent the offense from scoring. In addition, the defense tries to make the offensive team give up possession of the ball as far as possible from the goal line it is defending.

Offenses and defenses have many strategic options available to accomplish these objectives. Read unit 8 for information on how to teach your team basic offensive and defensive tactics.

What's the Score?

Play	Points	Description
Touchdown	6	Player in control of ball touches vertical plane of opponent's goal line
Field goal	3	Placekick or dropkick from scrimmage that, without touching the ground, goes through uprights of goal; no dropkick allowed in flag and touch football
Point after touchdown	2	Run, pass, or placekick from the 10-yard line*
Point after touchdown	1	Run, pass, or placekick from the 3-yard line
Safety	2	Offensive player is tackled or loses ball out of bounds in his own end zone
		Offensive player has flag pulled or is touched in his own end zone

In USFTL flag and touch football, 2 points instead of 1 are awarded for successful PATs from the 10-yard line to encourage the development of kicking skills in young players.

What Football Rules Should I Know?

Football rules are designed to make the game run smoothly and safely and prevent either team from gaining an unfair advantage. Throw out the rules, and a tackle football game quickly turns into a chaotic and dangerous competition where size, brute strength, and speed dominate.

Your league should already have rules concerning acceptable height and weight maximums and minimums for players. Even so, make sure your kids are matched up against opponents with similar physiques and skills. Discourage players from cutting weight to be eligible for your team. And, if you spot a mismatch during a game, talk with the opposing coach to see if you can cooperate and correct the problem.

Your league will also specify the length of your games. Typically, youth tackle football games consist of four 8- or 10-minute quarters. The clock is stopped when

- there is a change of possession,
- the ball goes out of bounds,
- an incomplete pass is thrown,
- the yard markers need to be advanced after a team gains 10 yards for a first down,
- a player is injured and officials call a time-out,
- a team scores, or
- a team calls a time-out.

You will be given two or three time-outs in each half. Use them wisely, not just for talking strategy. Remember, although the games may seem short to you, young players can easily become fatigued. So, besides substituting regularly, call a time-out when you see that your team is tired.

The time of games for flag and touch football are two 24-minute halves. The clock runs continuously for the first 22 minutes of each half and stops only for time-outs and scores. After the 2-minute warning, the clock stops for each event that it stops for in tackle football. Three time-outs per half are allowed, but you must use one of your time-outs before the 2-minute warning or you lose it.

Playing by the Rules

You are in a position to teach your players more than simply obeying the rules of the game. As a coach, you have a responsibility to teach them only those techniques that are safe.

For example, in tackle football you must, of course, discourage spearing on defense; that's against the rules. But it's also essential to teach young players *never* to lead with their heads when blocking or running. Kicking or striking an opponent or jumping on the pile at the conclusion of a play is not acceptable. Also, teach your players not to grasp an opponent's face mask because doing so can cause serious neck injuries. If you fail to do so, you are directly contributing not only to the next penalty one of your players commits but also to the next injury one of your players suffers.

Tackle football is a contact, perhaps collision, sport. If participants play according to the letter and spirit of the rules, youngsters can participate safely. Make certain that your players do. The proper football techniques to teach young football players are described in unit 7. "Tackle Football No-Nos" and "Flag and Touch Football No-Nos" list the techniques that you should not tolerate.

TACKLE FOOTBALL NO-NOS

It's inevitable that your players will violate minor rules during practices and games; even pros go offside now and then. But make clear to your players that some actions are unacceptable on the football field. Officials typically call unsportsmanlike conduct penalties or personal fouls for these actions.

✗ Tripping
✗ Face masking (pulling on an opponent's face mask)
✗ Blocking or tackling with a closed fist
✗ Spearing (tackling with top of helmet)
✗ Swearing
✗ Taunting
✗ Fighting
✗ Clipping (blocking a player in the back)
✗ Clotheslining (knocking a player down with a blow to the head or neck)

FLAG AND TOUCH FOOTBALL NO-NOS

✗ Illegally secured flag belt
✗ Spiking, kicking, throwing, or not returning the ball to the official during dead ball
✗ Hurdling
✗ Driving or running into a player
✗ Two-on-one blocking
✗ Tackling a runner
✗ Roughing the passer
✗ Illegal contact
✗ Tripping
✗ Swearing
✗ Taunting
✗ Fighting
✗ Clipping
✗ Contact with anything but open, extended arms

Promote good sportsmanship along with the use of proper fundamentals. Encourage players to help opponents up from the ground after a play. Ask ballcarriers to hand the ball to the referee or leave it on the ground where they were stopped. The official will appreciate such behavior, and so will the players' parents, league administrators, and players' future coaches.

Common Rule Infractions

The United States Flag and Touch Football League, Pop Warner Football, and your local youth football program have rule books available for your use. Take the time to study and learn the ins and outs, and then teach the rules to your football team.

Although no youth football team will perform penalty free, teach your players to avoid recurring penalties. By instilling this discipline, you'll help them enjoy more success, both as individuals and as a team.

Here is a brief list of common infractions that football players commit.

Offside: Defensive player in or beyond the neutral zone when the ball is snapped

Encroachment: Offensive player in or beyond the neutral zone before the ball is snapped

Illegal procedure: Failure of the offensive team to have seven players on the line of scrimmage (in 11-man football); failure of offensive teams to have four players on the line of scrimmage at the snap (in 8-man flag and touch football); the offensive team having more than one player in motion or a player moving toward the line of scrimmage before the snap

Delay of game: Offensive team taking more than 25 seconds to snap the ball after the referee has marked it ready for play

Holding: Any player using the arms to hook or lock up an opponent to impede his movement; an offensive player extending the arms outside his body frame to grab an opponent

Pass interference (defensive): Defensive player making contact with an eligible receiver who is beyond the neutral zone with the intent of impeding the offensive player trying to catch a catchable forward pass

As you teach your athletes to play with discipline and to avoid such rule violations, remember that you are their model. Players will reflect the discipline that you display in teaching them in practices and coaching them from the sidelines during games. So show respect for the rules, and don't shrug off game infractions or personal misconduct. And provide a great example by communicating respectfully with the individuals who officiate your games.

Officiating

Football rules are enforced by a crew of officials on the field. From the opening coin toss to the final horn, officials see to it that the game is conducted fairly.

In youth tackle football, as many as seven officials or as few as two may work the games. The referee is the official who controls the game, marking the ball ready for play; signaling penalties, time-outs, and first downs; and communicating with team captains and coaches. Appendix B shows referees' signals for the most common rule infractions.

If you have a concern about how a game is being officiated, address the referee respectfully. Do so immediately if at any time you feel that the officiating jeopardizes the safety of your players.

Player Positions

Give your young athletes a chance to play a variety of positions, on both offense and defense. By playing different positions, they'll become better all-around players and will probably stay more interested in the sport. Furthermore, they'll have a better understanding of the many skills and tactics used in the game. They will also better appreciate the efforts of their teammates who play positions they find difficult.

Offensive Positions in Tackle Football

Figure 6.6 illustrates a basic 11-player offensive alignment. Here's a brief outline of the desired attributes and responsibilities of players at each position.

Offensive Linemen

Ideally, you'll be able to put big, strong, and quick athletes into the center, guard, and tackle positions. These players must block and open up holes for ballcarriers to run through. When a pass play is called, they must protect the quarterback from opposing linemen.

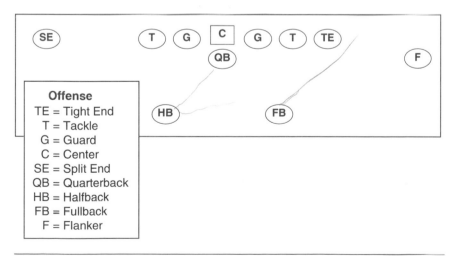

■ **Figure 6.6**　Offensive team alignment for tackle football.

Receivers

Another player who has important blocking duties is the tight end, positioned on the line of scrimmage, next to (within 3 yards of) either tackle. The tight end must be strong enough to block a defensive end, yet speedy enough to get open on pass routes.

The two other receiver positions are the flanker and the split end, or wide receiver. Speed and agility, along with great catching ability, are the qualities to look for in filling these spots. The flanker can be positioned on either side, off the line of scrimmage, whereas the split end is 8 to 10 yards outside the opposite tackle and up on the line. When the flanker is on the split end side, he is referred to as the slot. When a team positions a split end and flanker on each side of the line, it's called a double slot.

Quarterback

Lined up directly behind the center to receive the snap, the quarterback is the field general of the offense. The quarterback calls the plays in the huddle, barks out the snap count at the line of scrimmage, and then, after taking the snap, hands the ball off, runs with it, or passes it.

At this position you'll want a good communicator and good athlete who can handle many responsibilities. To complete your wish list, the quarterback will have an excellent throwing arm.

Running Backs

Most teams use a two-back set, either a deuce formation like the one shown in figure 6.6 or an I formation in which the backs line up in a straight line behind the quarterback.

Often, one running back is called a fullback and the other a halfback. The fullback has more blocking responsibilities and is expected to pick up short yardage when needed. Therefore, you'll want a strong, fairly fast, and dependable player at this position. The halfback (called the tailback in the I formation) is the primary ballcarrier. Speed and agility to outrun and outmaneuver would-be tacklers are desirable attributes for a halfback.

Some coaches prefer to line up their teams in a three-back set, moving the flanker to a wingback (WB) (see figure 6.7) in the single-wing formation or to a second halfback position to form a wishbone alignment (see figure 6.8). Coaches typically use the single-wing and wishbone formations when they want their teams to run the ball much more than pass it.

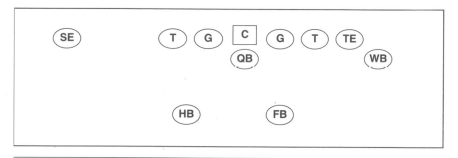

■ **Figure 6.7** Single-wing formation.

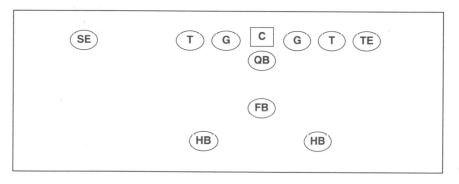

■ **Figure 6.8** Wishbone formation.

Offensive Positions in Flag and Touch Football

Figure 6.9 illustrates a basic eight-player offensive alignment. In flag and touch football, all players are eligible receivers. Here's a brief outline of the desired attributes and responsibilities of players at each position.

Quarterback

The quarterback lines up 5 to 15 yards behind the center in the offensive backfield, in what is sometimes called the shotgun formation. He should have the same attributes as a quarterback in tackle football.

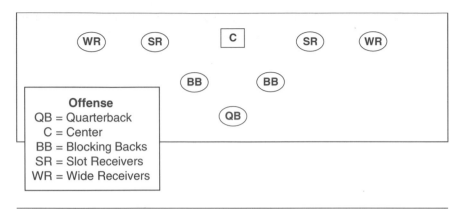

■ **Figure 6.9**   Offensive team alignment for flag and touch football.

Center

The center lines up on the line of scrimmage and is an eligible pass receiver in flag and touch football. He must be able to snap the ball back to the quarterback in a shotgun formation with speed and accuracy.

Blocking Backs

The blocking backs are eligible pass receivers, lined up in the offensive back field about 3 to 5 yards from the line of scrimmage. Their job is to protect the quarterback and receive passes. They also may be split out to "flood" a side of the field with several receivers.

Slot Receivers

The slot receivers take positions halfway between the center and the wide receivers. They must be fast and agile with good receiving abilities.

Wide Receivers

The wide receivers take positions on the outside ends of the line of scrimmage. They are usually the team's fastest players who can also run good patterns and have good hands.

The spread formation (see figure 6.10) is used to spread a defense and make it possible for the quarterback to find a "hot," or wide-open, receiver.

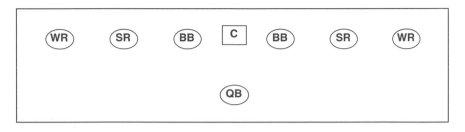

■ **Figure 6.10** Spread formation for flag and touch football.

The triple-wing formation (see figure 6.11) is used when a team has more than one good quarterback. This formation creates a wide-open style of offense by making the defense uncertain about who will throw the ball.

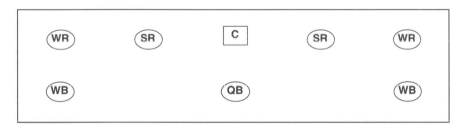

■ **Figure 6.11** Triple-wing formation for flag and touch football.

Defensive Positions in Tackle Football

Now it's time to look at the players you'll be asking to stop the opposing team from moving the football. Here are the basic defensive positions, with a short discussion of the skills and duties of each one.

Defensive Linemen

Youth football coaches put four to six players up front, on the line. The four-man front consists of two tackles and two ends. The five-man front adds a nose guard in the middle; the six-man front adds two ends who start in an upright position, much like outside linebackers (see next section).

Defensive tackles and defensive ends are primarily responsible for finding out who has the football and tackling him before he can gain yardage. It is also their duty to rush the passer when the offense attempts to throw the ball. To carry out their assignments, it is helpful for defensive linemen to have adequate size and strength as well as great quickness to fend off or avoid blocks by offensive players.

Linebackers

Depending on the number of linemen you use, you will want two to four linebackers on defense. No matter how many you use, each should have a nose for the ball—that is, he should be able to read the offense's play and stop it quickly.

The standard three-linebacker set shown in figure 6.12 complements the four-man front nicely. In this alignment, you have a middle linebacker at the heart of the defense and two outside linebackers.

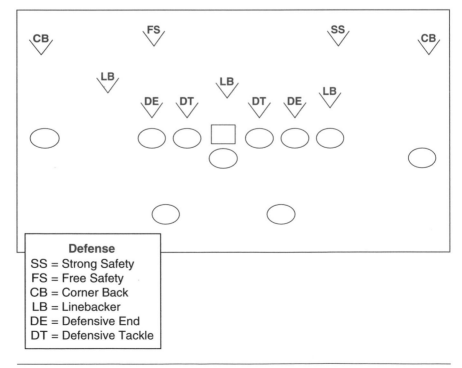

Defense
SS = Strong Safety
FS = Free Safety
CB = Corner Back
LB = Linebacker
DE = Defensive End
DT = Defensive Tackle

■ **Figure 6.12** Defensive team alignment for tackle football.

The middle linebacker should be one of your best athletes and surest tacklers. The outside linebacker on the tight end side, often called Sam for short to indicate that he plays on the offense's *strong side*, must be strong enough to fend off blocks but also fast enough to cover the tight end on pass routes. Will, the weakside linebacker, must be able to stand his ground against blocks by linemen and backs to prevent the offense from running the ball successfully.

Defensive Backs

The players responsible for preventing long runs and completed passes by the offense are the defensive backs. Again, depending on the alignment of your defensive front, the offense's set, and the game situation, you'll have three to five defensive backs in the game. Safeties have run and pass responsibilities. Cornerbacks cover the wide-outs.

All of these players must be agile and fast to cover speedy receivers. In addition, the safeties must be good tacklers to assist linebackers in stopping the run.

Defensive Positions in Flag and Touch Football

Here's a short discussion of the skills and duties of the basic defensive positions in flag and touch football (see figure 6.13).

Defensive End

The defensive ends are strong and quick players who rush the quarterback.

Nose Tackle

The nose tackle is a strong, quick player who rushes the quarterback and stops the run.

Linebacker

Linebackers usually captain the defense and call defensive signals. They must be strong and quick with a keen sense of timing because they are in the middle of almost every play on defense.

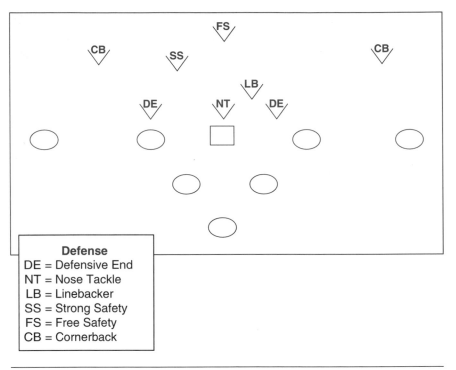

■ Figure 6.13 Defensive team alignment for flag and touch football.

Strong Safety

The strong safety is a defensive back who can double as a linebacker in certain defenses. He must be quick, agile, and strong enough to be able to cover and react to the ball.

Free Safety

The free safety is positioned at the deepest point of the defense. He is the last man between the defense and the goal line. He must be a very smart player because his primary responsibility is to read and go to the ball. He must also be fast.

Cornerback

The cornerbacks must be the fastest players on defense because it is their responsibility to cover the fastest players on offense, the wide receivers. They must be able to read and react, but they must also be able to come up in certain situations if the offense is trying a trick play, such as a double pass or an end around.

Special-Teams Positions for Tackle Football

Besides assigning players to the basic offensive and defensive spots, you'll need to designate players for special-teams positions. Here is a quick look at the key positions on each unit for tackle football.

Punt and Kick Teams

Long snapper: Center on field goal and punt teams

Holder: Player who receives snap on field goal attempts and places the ball on the tee for the kicker

Kicker: Kicker on kickoff, field goal, and PAT teams (see figure 6.14)

Punter: Kicker on punt team

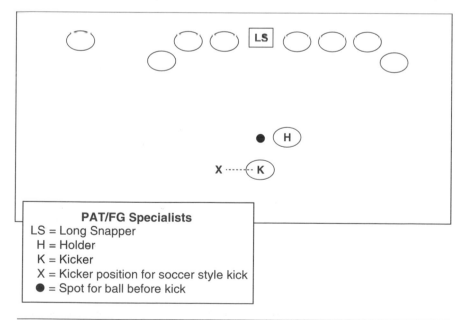

PAT/FG Specialists
LS = Long Snapper
H = Holder
K = Kicker
X = Kicker position for soccer style kick
● = Spot for ball before kick

■ **Figure 6.14**   Alignment for a PAT or field goal.

Punt and Kickoff Return Teams

Kick returner: Player farthest from kicker, whom the kickoff return team most wants to field and run with the ball

Punt returner: Player farthest from punter, whom the punt return team most wants to field and run with the ball

Special-Teams Positions for Flag and Touch Football

Here's a quick look at the key positions for flag and touch football special teams.

Punt Teams

Center: Player who snaps the ball back to the punter in a rapid and accurate motion

Punter: The kicker on the punt team

Linemen: Players who go down and pull the flag or touch the kick returner (see figure 6.15)

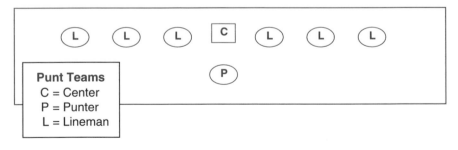

■ **Figure 6.15** Punt team alignment for flag and touch football.

Kickoff Teams

Safety back: Player on a kickoff team responsible for stopping an opposing player who breaks a long return

Kicker: Kicker on kickoff teams

Linemen: Players who go down and pull the flag or touch the kick returner

Kickoff Return Teams

Kick returner: Player farthest from kicker, whom the kickoff return team most wants to field and run with the ball

Upback: Player who blocks for kick returner and sometimes returns short kick; field general of return teams who calls the directions of the returns

Linemen: Players who block for kick returns (see figure 6.16)

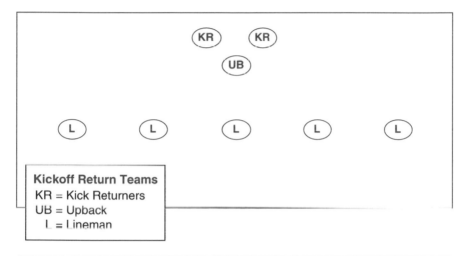

■ **Figure 6.16** Kickoff return team alignment for flag and touch football.

Punt Return Teams

Punt returner: Player farthest from punter, whom the punt return team most wants to field and run with the ball

Upback: Player who blocks for punt returners, sometimes returns short punts; field general of return teams who calls the directions for the returners

Linemen: Players who block for punt returners

Extra Point and Field Goal Teams

Placekicker: Kicker on kickoff, field goal, and PAT teams

Holder: Player who receives snap on field goal attempts and places the ball on the tee for the kicker

Center: Player who snaps ball on field goal and extra point teams

Floater: Player who calls the plays on field goals and extra point attempts; lines up wherever he sees the most need, perhaps to help block on one side; may also call for a fake field goal or extra point

Guard: Player who blocks for kicker and holder; lines up next to center

Tackle: Player who blocks for kicker and holder; lines up next to guard on outside of line (see figure 6.17)

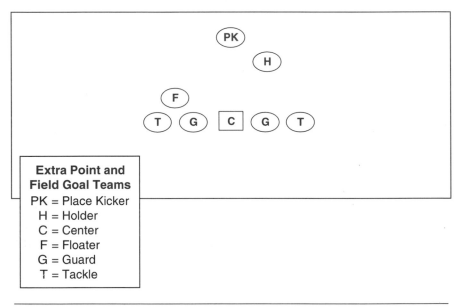

Extra Point and
Field Goal Teams
PK = Place Kicker
 H = Holder
 C = Center
 F = Floater
 G = Guard
 T = Tackle

■ **Figure 6.17** Extra point and field goal team alignment for flag and touch football.

Football Terms to Know

Tackle Football

audible—Using a vocal signal at the line of scrimmage to change the play previously called in the huddle.

backfield—Players who are legally behind the scrimmage line when the ball is snapped.

blitz—When a defense commits extra players, in addition to line-men, to rush the passer.

chains—Ten-yard length of chain used to measure distance required for a first down.

cross block—Two linemen blocking defenders who are diagonally opposite the blockers' own starting positions; one of the blockers moves first.

defensive formation—An alignment of defensive linemen, lineback-ers, and defensive backs positioned to stop a particular offense.

downs—A series of four consecutive charged scrimmages allotted to the offensive team; to retain possession the offense must ad-vance the ball to a yard line called the necessary line during these scrimmages.

eligible receiver—Any offensive player who is legally in the backfield or any player on either end of the line of scrimmage.

end zone—That area bounded by the goal line, end line, and sidelines.

even defense—A defense having an even number of linemen.

fair catch—The unhindered catch by a member of the receiving team of any kick that has crossed the kicking team's line of scrimmage or free-kick line, provided the proper signal (that is, one hand and arm extended above the head and moving them side to side) has been given by the receiver.

field goal—A placekick or dropkick from scrimmage that goes through the uprights of the goal without touching the ground first. Three points are awarded for a field goal.

first down—The first of four allotted downs the offensive team re-ceives, occurring when the offensive team gains 10 or more yards within its allotted four downs.

forward pass—A pass that strikes anything beyond the spot from which the pass is thrown; a pass in the direction of the opponents' goal.

fumble—A player's losing possession of the football other than by passing or kicking it.

goal line defense—Defensive alignment used near the defensive team's own goal line and sometimes in short yardage situations (e.g., third and one) that places defensive linemen in the six gaps and has all defensive players close to the line of scrimmage in an attempt to stop the anticipated running plan.

goal post—A structure placed on each end line of the field; attempts at field goals and extra points must pass through the goal posts to be successful.

handoff—The ball being handed (not passed or lateraled) from one player to another. The quarterback usually executes a handoff to a running back, but a running back might also execute a handoff to the receiver of a reverse.

hash mark—Line running the length of the field bisecting the yard lines. The ball is not placed outside the hash marks when a play is to begin.

I formation—Offensive formation in which a fullback and tailback are positioned in a line directly behind the quarterback—the center, quarterback, fullback, and tailback form an "I."

illegal use of hands—With possession of the ball established by either team, a player's using the hands to grasp and impede an opponent who is not a ballcarrier.

ineligible receiver—A player on the line of scrimmage (with at least one other player on either side of him) who cannot legally catch a pass or—on a pass play—be downfield before a pass is thrown.

interception—Gaining possession of the ball; occurs when a defender catches a pass thrown by the offense.

kickoff—A free kick initiating each half of play; it follows the scoring of a field goal or extra point. The ball is either placed on the kicking team's 40-yard line in a kicking tee or held by a player on the kicking team. All players on the kicking team must remain behind their 40-yard line until the ball is kicked. Once the ball travels 10 yards downfield, either team can establish position. ·

kickoff return—The team receiving a kickoff establishes possession of the ball and attempts to advance the ball upfield.

late hit—An infraction occurring when a player hits an opponent after the whistle has already blown the play dead.

lateral pass—When the ball is tossed or thrown backward. (If it is dropped, it is considered a fumble.)

line of scrimmage—An imaginary line running perpendicular to the sidelines. The offensive and defensive lines of scrimmage are located on either end of the neutral zone and mark the ball's position at the start of each down.

man-to-man coverage—Defensive pass coverage in which defenders are assigned specific receivers to cover; they cover those receivers no matter where they run their routes.

neutral zone— Area located within the width of the football.

odd defense—Defense in which a player is lined up on the center.

offensive formation—The offensive team's lineup; that is, the locations of the offensive players before the snap of the ball.

onside kick—A play in which a kickoff is deliberately made short, so that the team kicking off has a better opportunity to get possession of the ball.

option—An offensive play designed to give the ballcarrier the opportunity to carry the ball upfield, hand the ball off, or pass it to a teammate.

passing route—The path a receiver takes in an attempt to get open to receive a pass (or to serve as a decoy).

pass rush—A defender's attempt to tackle or harry a member of the offensive team attempting to pass the football.

placekick—A play in which the ball is kicked from a tee or from the hold of a member of the kicking team, used for field goals and kickoffs.

play-action pass—A play in which a fake handoff precedes a pass attempt   this kind of pass is designed to pull in the linebackers and defensive backs and to slow the pass rush (by making the defense think the play is a run).

possession—Having control of the ball.

punt—Kicking the ball after dropping it and before it reaches the ground. Offensive teams who have failed to cover 10 yards in their first three attempts often use a punt on the fourth down.

punt coverage—When a ball is punted, players of the punting team running downfield in an attempt to tackle an opponent who has fielded the punted ball and not called for a fair catch.

punt return—A player who has received a punted ball tries to advance it.

quarterback sneak—A quarterback running or diving over the line of scrimmage.

roughing the passer—An infraction that occurs when a defensive player hits the quarterback after the ball has been released. The official must decide whether the defensive player had time to stop after the ball's release.

sack—The action of a defender tackling the quarterback behind the line of scrimmage.

shotgun—An offensive formation in which the quarterback is lined up in the backfield about 5 to 7 yards behind the center.

snap—The quick exchange of the football from the center to the quarterback to put the ball into play.

T formation—An offensive formation in which the fullback is positioned 2 to 4 yards behind a quarterback who is positioned immediately behind the center. One halfback is on either side of the fullback, and the fullback and the two halfbacks are in a line parallel with the line of scrimmage.

time-out—The clock's being stopped at the request of a player of either team. In general, each team is allowed three such requests during each half of a game.

touchback— Balls kicked through the end zone or downed in the receiving team's end zone. The referee then places the ball on the receiving team's 20-yard line for it to start from.

trap block—Technique in which an offensive lineman pulls out of the line and blocks an unsuspecting defender elsewhere down the line.

two-point conversion—Successfully running or passing the ball into the end zone from the 3-yard line following a touchdown.

wishbone—An offensive formation in which the quarterback is under center (direct snap), a fullback is directly behind the quarterback, and two halfbacks are behind and to the sides of the fullback.

zone coverage—Defensive pass coverage in which defenders are assigned specific areas to cover and cover anyone coming into these areas.

Flag and Touch Football

contact blocking—Open-hand, straight-arm blocking between two players. Contact above the shoulders or below the waist is not permitted. Players may not leave their feet to block.

deflagging—The legal removal of a flag from an opponent in possession of the ball. Pushing, striking, holding, slapping, or tripping when attempting to pull a flag is not permitted. Defensive players may leave their feet to pull a flag. Offensive players are not permitted to protect or guard their flags.

flag football—Played between two teams of eight players each. Six players are required to avoid a forfeit. The type of blocking that is used is contact blocking. All players are eligible receivers.

flag removal—When the flag is clearly taken from the runner, the down is over and the ball is declared dead. A player who removes the flag from the runner should immediately hold the flag above his head to assist the official in locating the spot where the capture occurred. If a flag inadvertently falls to the ground, a two-hand tag between the shoulders and knees constitutes capture.

fumble—There are no fumbles in flag and touch football. Once the ball hits the ground during a play, it is ruled dead at the spot.

ineligible lineman flag football—Played between two teams of nine players each. Seven players are required to avoid a forfeit. The type of blocking that is used is contact blocking. The center and the two players on either side of the center (guards) are ineligible to receive a forward pass or run with the ball. All other players are eligible to receive.

number of players needed to avoid a forfeit—The number of players needed to start a game and avoid a forfeit are as follows:

> 2-man team—2 players needed
> 3-man team—2 players needed
> 4-man team—2 players needed
> 5-man team—3 players needed
> 6-man team—4 players needed
> 7-man team—5 players needed
> 8-man team—6 players needed
> 9-man team—7 players needed
> 10-man team—8 players needed
> 11-man team—9 players needed

protected scrimmage kick—A punt. The punting team may request that the defense not rush until the ball is punted.

screen blocking—A form of blocking with no contact between players. The player's arms must be at his side when making a screen block. Players may not leave their feet to screen block.

screen flag football—Played between two teams of seven players each. Five players are required to avoid a forfeit. The type of blocking that is used is screen blocking. All players are eligible receivers.

touch football—Played between two teams of seven players each. Five players are required to avoid a forfeit. The type of blocking that is used is contact blocking. All players are eligible receivers.

touching—Simultaneous placing of both hands anywhere between the shoulders and knees of an opponent who has the ball. This includes the ball in the ballcarrier's possession. The feet of the toucher may leave the ground to make a touch. Pushing, striking, slapping, and holding are not permitted. Tripping the ballcarrier in an attempt to make a diving tag results in a penalty.

zone line to gain—The next line on the playing field in the direction of, and parallel to, the opponent's goal line. The down box is stationed at the zone line to gain.

What Football Skills and Drills Should I Teach?

To participate successfully in tackle football, a player must be able to get in the proper stance and must be able to block and tackle. The skills used in flag and touch football are essentially the same as those used in tackle football without, of course, the tackling and physical play. Flag or touch football is more of an aerobic sport, but it uses most aspects of tackle football—receiving, running, and noncontact blocking, to name a few. Flag or touch football also lets large children play against small children with no advantages for either child. This unit describes how to teach football techniques. It also explains skills specific to various positions and outlines selected drills that will help players develop them.

It is important that you understand the skills of football and teach them properly. To improve their level of play and success, players must execute the skills of the game properly. Start out by teaching the basics of a skill and progress only when the players are able to perform the skill. Most football skills are not natural actions, so you should continue to review the basics with your players every time you practice. If your players are not successful in performing a technique, you can probably trace it back to difficulty with one of the basic skills. For example, if your offensive lineman is getting beaten on his pass protection, he is probably standing too erect. You need to practice with him the basic stance, the initial step, and the proper body position for pass protection. Teams that learn the proper skills and techniques and are able to perform them in a game will win most contests.

OFFENSIVE SKILLS

When you tell your players that it's time to work on offensive skills, the first thing that will pop into their minds is "touchdown." So you have to explain to them that TDs happen only when every offensive player properly executes the techniques of his position within the team's strategy. In this section you'll learn how to instruct your players in these important, basic offensive skills.

Stance

The stance is the proper alignment of a player's body to start each play. Following is a description of the stances you should teach players at each position.

Offensive Linemen

Before the snap, offensive linemen should take a three-point stance. Figure 7.1 illustrates how this stance should look. Use these points to teach the correct stance to tackles, guards, and centers:

✔ Place the feet shoulder-width apart, in a heel-instep relationship, with the dominant foot back.
✔ Put very little weight on the down hand to allow for quick forward, backward, and lateral movement.
✔ Place your left arm loosely across your left thigh.
✔ Keep your back straight, with your head up to see defenders across the line of scrimmage. This position is the strongest and safest for the back and neck.

■ **Figure 7.1** Proper three-point stance for an offensive lineman.

Receivers

In both tackle football and flag and touch football, wide receivers and slot receivers (touch and flag) use two basic types of stances. The first is a three-point stance, in which the receiver distributes his weight evenly, with his head up and his eyes focused either directly downfield or on the football (see figure 7.2). His feet are staggered, which allows for good explosion from the line of scrimmage. The second stance used by the wide receiver is a two-point or upright stance (see figure 7.3). Its advantages are that the receiver can get off the line of scrimmage without being held up, and that he is in immediate position to receive quick passes.

Three-Point Stance

- ✔ Place the feet shoulder-width apart, in a heel-toe relationship, with the foot closest to the football staggered in a comfortable sprinter's position.
- ✔ Point knees and toes straight ahead.
- ✔ Keep your back straight, parallel to the ground, and your head up.

Two-Point Stance

- ✔ Place the feet shoulder-width apart, in a heel-toe relationship, with the foot closest to the football back slightly more than the other.
- ✔ Bend knees in a comfortable position.
- ✔ Keep weight on the balls of your feet.
- ✔ Keep your back straight, leaning forward slightly.
- ✔ Square your shoulders to the line of scrimmage.
- ✔ Hold your arms in a comfortable position.

Center

In flag and touch football, the center is an eligible pass receiver. He must be able to snap the ball back to the quarterback in a quick and accurate motion that will give the quarterback an extra second or two to read the defense and make a pass attempt or run with the

■ **Figure 7.2** Three-point stance for receivers.

■ **Figure 7.3** Two-point stance for receivers.

ball. The center must also be an excellent receiver because he is in the center of the field and is involved in many pass plays. The center is considered the tailback or workhorse of the offense in flag and touch football. The center must also be able to pass protect on some occasions. He should use a three-point stance with his head looking under his spread legs at the quarterback (see figure 7.4).

✔ Place your feet shoulder-width apart in a heel-toe relationship, with the foot closest to the football staggered in a comfortable sprinter's position.

✔ Point knees and toes straight ahead.

✔ Keep your back straight, parallel to the ground, with your head looking back under your spread legs at the quarterback.

■ **Figure 7.4** Three-point stance for center in flag and touch football.

Wingback

In flag and touch football, the wingback is a quarterback and wide receiver combined. He must possess all the skills of a wide receiver and quarterback to excel at the position. The proper stance for a wingback is a two-point stance, positioned at the far wings in the offensive backfield, about 10 yards off the line of scrimmage.

- ✔ Bend your knees in a comfortable position.
- ✔ Keep weight on the balls of your feet.
- ✔ Keep your back straight, leaning forward slightly.
- ✔ Square your shoulders to the line of scrimmage.
- ✔ Hold your arms in a comfortable position.

Quarterback

A quarterback's stance must be poised and relaxed, reflecting confidence. The quarterback's feet should be comfortably spread, approximately shoulder-width apart, and, in tackle football, as close to the center's feet as possible. He should bend his knees slightly and drop his hips while remaining as tall over the center as possible. The quarterback's shoulders should be parallel to the line of scrimmage, his head up to check the positioning of the defense (see figure 7.5).

■ **Figure 7.5** Quarterback's stance from the front and the side.

In flag and touch football, which are primarily passing games, the quarterback usually stands in a shotgun formation to receive the snap. This gives the quarterback the advantage of being able to see the entire field and helps him separate from the line of scrimmage, which gives him more time to throw.

Running Backs

The most common stance for halfbacks and fullbacks is a two-point stance (see figure 7.6). Players at these positions need to accelerate quickly from their backfield spot. Teach them to use the following stance before the ball is snapped:

- ✔ Place your feet about shoulder-width apart with your weight on the balls of your feet.
- ✔ Keep your feet nearly parallel for a quick burst in any direction.
- ✔ Bend your knees slightly with your hands on your knees.
- ✔ Keep your head up with eyes looking ahead.

If your running backs will be using the three-point stance, teach them the same stance technique you taught the offensive linemen.

■ **Figure 7.6** Two-point stance for the running back.

Blocking Backs

In flag and touch football, blocking backs have two roles—protecting the quarterback and receiving passes. They must be able to do both well. Blocking backs should start out in a two-point stance so that they can see oncoming defensive players. A two-point stance also enables a blocking back to release quickly into a pass pattern. Blocking backs need to accelerate quickly from their backfield spot. Teach them to use the stance you taught the running backs.

✔ Place your feet about shoulder-width apart with your weight on the balls of your feet.
✔ Keep your feet nearly parallel for a quick burst in any direction.
✔ Bend your knees slightly with your hands on your knees.
✔ Keep your head up with eyes looking ahead.

Stance Drills

Name.   Ready Stance Drill

Purpose.   To teach proper stance.

Organization.   Players line up, each in the proper stance for his position. You inspect each player's stance, making necessary corrections. Then the players fire out for 5 yards and properly execute a designated skill from the stance. Be aware of body position as the players come out of their stances.

Coaching Points.   By learning the correct stance and developing good initial movement, your players will become more efficient. Young players have a tendency to rush right into performing the skill, so stress the importance of proper setup and a quick first step.

Blocking

Blocking is the cornerstone of all successful offensive teams. Teams use blocking to move a defensive man out of the area where they want to run the football and to keep defensive linemen from tackling, touching, or pulling the flag of the quarterback.

In tackle football, offensive linemen block in some manner on every play. Running backs block when they are not carrying the football, and wide receivers block when they are not catching the football. In flag and touch football, blocking backs block on every play. Wide receivers block when they are not catching the ball. For tackle football, teach your players three types of blocks: the drive block, the downfield block, and the pass protection block. In flag and touch football, there are two main types of blocking: contact and screen. All blocking in flag and touch football is done from a two-point stance with an open-hand, straight-arm approach.

Drive Block

The drive block is a one-on-one block used most often when a defensive lineman lined up directly over an offensive man must be moved for the play to succeed. When teaching your tackle football players the drive block, emphasize these points (see figure 7.7):

- ✔ Explode from your stance with the foot closest to the opponent and drive your hips forward on the third and fourth steps, through the block.
- ✔ Start with short, choppy steps, and keep your feet moving.
- ✔ Deliver the block from a wide base, and keep your head up and shoulders square.
- ✔ Punch hands or forearms into the opponent to establish momentum, and deliver the blow on impact with the forearms, not the head.
- ✔ Keep your head on the side of the opponent toward the hole, and follow through with short, choppy steps, turning the opponent away from the hole.

If you teach your flag and touch football players the drive block, emphasize these points (see figure 7.8):

- ✔ Start with short, choppy steps and keep your feet moving, your head up, and your hands and arms out in front of your body to keep the defensive man away from you.
- ✔ Deliver the block from a wide base and keep your head up and shoulders square.

✔ Keep your head on the side of the opponent toward the hole, and follow through with short, choppy steps, turning the opponent away from the hole.

■ **Figure 7.7** Proper drive blocking position for tackle football.

■ **Figure 7.8** Proper drive blocking position for flag and touch football.

Downfield Block

Teach your players two kinds of downfield blocks. In tackle football, a blocker should use the run-block technique when the ballcarrier is directly behind him. In this situation, he blocks the defender at full or three-quarter speed by attacking aggressively with the forearms and shoulders. In touch and flag football, the player blocks the defender at full or three-quarter speed with an arms-extended, open-palms approach to the upper body of his opponent.

The cross-body block is another common and effective block. Players may use this block from in front of the defender or from an angle to his side. To make this block, a player must throw one arm in front of the defender's head. This motion causes the defender to move his head back and expose his body. As part of the same movement, the blocker whips his body laterally and makes contact at the defender's midsection. The blocker then rolls his body into the defender to complete the block. Remind players never to cross-body block a defender below the waist when outside the zone of 4 yards on either side of the center and 3 yards on either side of the line of scrimmage.

Pass Protection Block

The pass protection block keeps the defender from getting to the quarterback before he can throw the football. Teach your running backs and your offensive linemen (in tackle football) and your blocking backs (in flag and touch football) the same technique for protecting the quarterback. Use the following sequential method to teach the pass protection block.

Initial Move and Setup

The initial move and setup technique is extremely important in pass blocking. In tackle football, the lineman must set up quickly, stepping with his inside foot first. The offensive lineman pushes up into a two-point stance with his down hand. The movement projects the offensive lineman into a position with his head up, eyes open wide, back straight, rear end down, hand and arms up, and feet positioned to move back or laterally in a split second. The depth behind the line of scrimmage should vary with the pass action called and the opponent's defensive front alignment.

The blocking back in flag and touch football uses the same technique except that he starts in a two-point stance with his hands on his knees.

Body Position

- ✔ Keep your head up and your rear end down.
- ✔ Keep your back straight.
- ✔ Place your feet shoulder-width apart, keep them moving, and flex your knees.
- ✔ Keep the weight of your body and head over your feet, never in front of them.

✔ Hold your elbows in with the hands, ready to ward off the challenge of the defensive lineman.

The lineman must position himself between the quarterback and the defensive pass rusher. He can do this by backing off the line of scrimmage quickly after the snap. Instruct your offensive linemen that they should never get beat to their inside.

The blocking back must also position himself between the quarterback and the defensive rusher. He can do this by backing off the line of scrimmage quickly after the snap or by setting up a few yards deep in the backfield before the snap.

Punch

Delivering a blow to stop the charge of the defensive lineman takes good timing. The player must let the defensive lineman get as close as six inches and then deliver the blow to stop the charge. The lineman or blocking back must strive to deliver a blow, step back away from the defensive lineman, and recoil. The player must deliver the punch with the elbows in close to the rib cage, locking the elbows and rolling the wrists to get power. No, we aren't recommending that you teach your linemen or blocking backs to throw left hooks at charging defenders. The linemen's or blocking backs' hands and arms must stay within the planes of the shoulders.

Patience

Patience may be the hardest thing to teach an offensive lineman or blocking back. He must be the protector, not the aggressor. He must keep his legs under him and always remain in a good blocking position even after delivering the punch. An effective coaching point is to instruct linemen or blocking backs to keep their rear ends down and their knees bent at all times.

Footwork

The most important skill for an offensive lineman or blocking back is the ability to move his feet. The correct foot movement is a shuffle, with the player keeping one foot always in contact with the ground. The linemen or blocking backs should never cross their feet and should keep their bodies parallel to the line of scrimmage with their backs always to the quarterback. Blockers should keep their feet shoulder-width apart. Figure 7.9 shows the proper position for pass protection.

■ **Figure 7.9** Proper position for pass protection.

Contact Blocking

Contact blocking in flag and touch football is legally hindering the progress of an opponent in a fair and safe way. Blockers must be on their feet before, during, and after they make contact with their opponent. In flag and touch football, the following play is not allowed anywhere on the field by a blocker:

- Diving to block
- Two-on-one blocking
- High-low block, cross-body block, or rolling block
- Grabbing the jersey of an opponent while attempting to block
- Locking the hands together
- Swinging, throwing, or flipping the elbow or forearm
- Contact of any kind to the head or shoulders

The blocker is allowed to contact the opponent's body only between the waist and shoulders. An open-hand, straight-arm block within the framework of the blocker's body is the ideal block to use to avoid unnecessary rough play. To keep contact blocking under control, stress safe, clean, sportsmanlike contact between opponents.

Screen Blocking

In flag and touch football, screen blocking is legally obstructing an opponent without contacting him with any part of the body. The screen blocker may have his hands and arms at the side or behind the back; any use of the arms, elbows, or legs to initiate contact during a screen block is illegal. A blocker may use his hands or arms to break a fall or retain his balance. A player must be on his feet before, during, and after screen blocking.

Several restrictions govern screen blocking:

1. When behind a stationary opponent, a screening player may not take a position closer than a normal step from him.

2. When assuming a position at the side or in front of a stationary opponent, a screening player may not make contact with him.

3. A screen blocker may not take a position so close to a moving opponent that the opponent cannot avoid contact by stopping or changing direction. The speed of the player to be screened will determine where the screener may take his stationary position. This position will vary and may be one or two normal steps or strides from the opponent.

4. After assuming a legal screening position, the screen blocker may not move to maintain it unless he moves in the same direction and path as the opponent. If the screener violates any of these provisions and contact results, he has committed a personal foul.

Blocking and Interlocked Interference

Teammates of a runner or passer may interfere for the player by screen blocking, but may not use interlocked interference by grasping or encircling one another in any manner.

Use of Hands or Arms by the Defense

Defensive players must go around the offensive player's screen block. They may not use the arms and hands as a wedge to contact the opponent. The application of this rule depends entirely on the judgment of the official. A blocker may use his arms or hands to break a fall or retain his balance.

Pass Protection Drills

Name.   Quick Set Drill

Purpose.   To get linemen or blocking backs quickly from their stance to a hitting position.

Organization.   The linemen or blocking backs line up in a circle in a good stance. On your command, they pop up into a correct pass protection position—taking a quick step with the inside foot, putting hands up in a punch position, and assuming a squat position, ready to strike a blow. To vary this drill, have them do this continuously for a minute—up, down, up, down.

Coaching Points.   To increase effort and avoid monotony, make the drill competitive. Call out quarterback signals and identify the lineman or blocking back who is quickest to get into the blocking position on the snap count.

Name.   Balance Drill

Purpose.   To help the linemen or blocking backs keep their feet apart and keep their bodies from being pushed, pulled, or tipped from side to side.

Organization.   The players line up across from each other and grab the shoulder pads (tackle football) or shoulder part of the jersey (flag and touch football) of the player opposite them. On your command, one of the partners, the defensive player, tries to get his opponent off balance by pushing, pulling, and tipping him from side to side. This forces the offensive player to get low, get a wide base, and move his feet to keep his balance. Switch partners and have players perform the drill again.

Coaching Points.   Correct errors in technique, such as not establishing a solid base and overextending the arms. Encourage defensive players to vary their attack and be active.

Name.   Punch Drill

Purpose.   To reinforce how players are to deliver a blow properly.

Organization.   Use a handheld pad (flag and touch football) or a punch board, a seven-man sled, blocking dummies, or teammates (tackle football). Players should start in an upright position and deliver the blow as they would against a defensive lineman—aim for the armpits, elbows in, squat position. Players should then extend the arms, locking the elbows and rolling the wrists to give extra power. Players then shuffle step to the next bag and repeat the technique.

Coaching Points.   Observe and correct players to make sure each punch is performed properly. Look for quick recovery and foot movement between blocks.

Name.   Screen-Blocking Drill

Purpose.   To teach proper noncontact screen-blocking fundamentals (see figure 7.10).

Organization.   Pair off players, with each defensive lineman rushing a blocking back in a one-on-one situation. The blocking back should keep his arms at his side and use a basketball pick to shield the quarterback, who lines up behind the blocking back. By moving his feet or shuffling with the defensive player, the blocking back can protect the quarterback without touching his opponent with his hands.

Coaching Points.   Observe and correct players to make sure all blocking backs are using their feet and bodies, not their arms and hands. Look for foot quickness. Encourage defensive players to try different approaches with their rushes, using, for example, a stutter step rush or a spin rush.

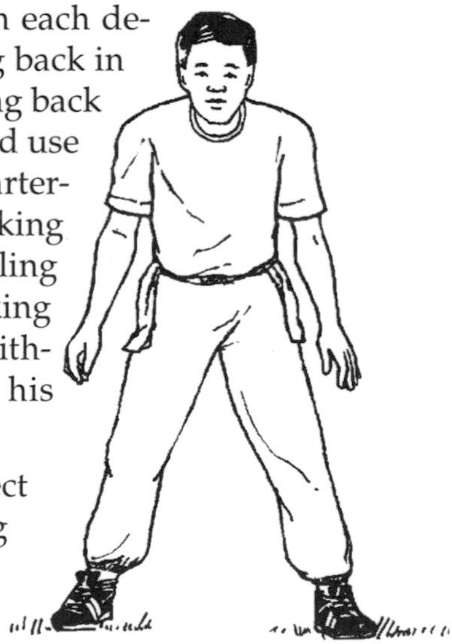

■ **Figure 7.10**   Proper position for a screen block in flag and touch football.

Name.   One-on-One Pass Protection

Purpose.   To put all the blocking techniques together in a live situation.

Organization.   Each offensive lineman faces a defensive lineman on the line of scrimmage. The quarterback calls the cadence, and on the snap of the football the offensive lineman sets up in a pass protection position and tries to prevent the defensive lineman from pressuring the quarterback.

Coaching Points.   Keep the number of offensive and defensive players down to three on a side. This will allow you to detect and correct mistakes to help the linemen improve. As players' skills progress, have the quarterback roll out to one side or the other, requiring the offensive linemen to protect a moving pocket.

Running the Football

Getting the Handoff

Instruct the running back that when he is getting the handoff from the quarterback, the elbow of his inside arm (the arm closest to the quarterback) should be up to receive the ball. He should bend the inside arm at the elbow (90-degree angle) and keep it parallel to the ground at about shoulder level. He should place the outside arm (the arm farthest from the quarterback) across the belt with the elbow close to the body, the palm of the hand turned up, and the fingers spread. Figure 7.11 shows a running back in proper handoff position. Allow your quarterback to place the football into the pocket formed by the running back.

Carrying the Football

After receiving the ball, the running back must protect it at all cost. Teach the ballcarrier to immediately tuck the end of the ball under his arm and cover the front point of the ball with his hand. The ball should be carried away from the pressure of the defense; that is,

■ **Figure 7.11**   Running back in proper handoff position.

when the ballcarrier is running to the right, the ball should be in his right arm with his hand over the point, and when he's running to the left, the ball should be in his left arm with his hand over the point. A coaching point is to carry the ball in the arm away from the inside linebacker.

Using Blockers

Coach your running backs to run toward the hole that has been called unless they see that the hole is closed. They should then head upfield to gain what yardage they can.

Teach them to run with a forward lean. This helps them to stay low and have a good forward drive.

Instruct the backs to make their cut at the last moment. They should approach the line of scrimmage with their shoulders square to the line. To prevent the defender from getting a solid tackle, a good running back will fake him by taking a step away from the defender, then cut back close to him as if he were cutting right through him. Coach each running back to set up his blockers by running on the blocker's outside hip, and then, at the last moment, cutting inside as the blocker takes out the defender.

▉ **Running Back Drill** ▉

Name.   Bag Drill

Purpose.   To teach players how to receive a proper handoff and keep the head up to make the correct read and cut.

Organization.   This drill involves the center, the quarterback, and the running backs. The quarterback takes the snap from the center and hands the football to the running back (check for proper handoff position of the arms). The back has his eyes upfield running toward a dummy (representing a defender) held 3 yards away by the coach (see figure 7.12). As the back approaches the dummy, the coach will move it to the right or the left, indicating that the back should cut in the opposite direction. Players should run at full speed to simulate game conditions. This drill helps players work on proper handoffs, hand placement on the football, and, for the running backs, change of direction.

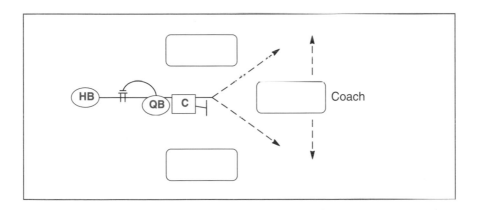

■ **Figure 7.12**   Bag Drill.

Coaching Points.   Emphasize quick and clean execution of the handoff. Watch runners to see that they plant and push off the foot that is on the side to which you point the bag. Emphasize to your players that defenders will recover unless the runner bursts at full speed in the opposite direction.

Playing Quarterback

Shotgun Formation

In flag and touch football, the quarterback starts in the shotgun formation (see figure 7.13). He lines up about 5 to 15 yards behind the center, depending on the particular play or the quarterback's arm strength. He should glance at the center and the line of scrimmage to make sure that he is at proper depth for the playcall. He should then look up at the defense and scan the field for particular defensive formations. That will enable him to see who might be open or alert him to call an audible if the defensive set indicates that a change of play is needed.

■ Figure 7.13 Quarterback receiving the snap in shotgun formation.

Taking the Snap From Under the Center

The quarterback should place his top hand, or pressure hand, so it pushes up on the center's rear end. This pressure tells the center where to snap the football. The quarterback should position the bottom hand, or catch hand, so the thumbs are together and the fingers extended, giving the center a good target for the ball. The quarterback should bend his elbows slightly to allow for the center's firing out on the snap.

At first the center should practice snapping the ball slowly to the quarterback, making sure he is getting it properly with the laces at or near the fingers of the throwing hand. The players should then practice at full speed. Spend five minutes each day on center-quarterback exchanges. Figure 7.14 illustrates a quarterback receiving the snap.

■ Figure 7.14 Quarterback receiving the snap.

The quarterback looks downfield, and when he receives the snap, he turns his head to see where he will hand off the ball. When he locates the target, he should keep his eyes on that player. On passing plays, he brings the football into his body at the belt and then raises it up to the armpit in a ready-to-throw position. The quarterback should not swing the football.

Footwork

The quarterback's initial pushoff begins when he receives the ball, never before. A transfer of weight must precede the pushoff; from a balanced position, the quarterback shifts his weight to the stable, or away, foot. His lead foot steps in the direction of the play in a swinging motion and must be kept close to the ground.

Handoff

The quarterback is completely responsible for the success or failure of the handoff. He must adjust to the running back's path and speed and get him the football.

Instruct the quarterback to keep both hands on the ball as long as possible and to lock the football into the pocket that the running back provides. Have him try to make the exchange with the foot on the same side as the give hand nearest the running back. Although not tremendously important, this allows for greater reach and balance. Coach your quarterback to place or press the ball firmly into the ballcarrier's pocket, allowing his give hand to ride the ball into place.

Dropback

After receiving the ball from the center, the quarterback usually takes three, five, or seven steps back, depending on the length of the receivers' routes. There are three types of drops—the crossover, the backpedal, and the rollout. The crossover involves bending the knees and lowering the rear end to begin movement and gain momentum. This first step (to the right for right-handed quarterbacks) should be parallel to the line of scrimmage, followed by several crossover steps to the setting point (see figure 7.15). In the last two steps before anchoring, the quarterback should shift his weight forward to slow up and should prepare to position his feet for the throw.

The backpedal begins with the same body position used in the crossover. The first step (with the right foot for right-handed quarterbacks), however, is directly backward, followed by a sequence of backpedals. Three-, five-, and seven-step drops are most common, allowing the quarterback to plant for the throw. Throughout the drop, the quarterback should keep his shoulders parallel to the line of scrimmage.

The rollout is a general term for any drop that involves the quarterback moving laterally to the line of scrimmage. The popular sprintout technique consists of the quarterback simply sprinting to a

■ **Figure 7.15** Quarterback in a crossover drop.

designated spot on one side of the field several yards behind the line of scrimmage. The bootleg is another rollout option, where the quarterback fakes a handoff to a back on one side of the field, then sprints in the opposite direction.

The crossover is the quickest and most conventional drop. The backpedal is slower but gives the quarterback more time to spot receivers and read the defense. The rollout is best for quick quarterbacks who can run the football and short quarterbacks who have trouble seeing downfield over tall linemen.

Throwing the Football

The quarterback keeps the ball in the ready position at the armpit before raising it straight up to throw. His elbow extends out and leads the ball toward the throw. He should grip the ball with the fingers over the laces and the index finger close to the tip of the football to guide it. There should be some space between the quarterback's palm and the football. He releases the ball with the thumb and the wrist facing down. On release, the index finger should be last to leave the football and should be pointed directly toward the target. Figure 7.16 shows the quarterback in proper throwing position.

■ **Figure 7.16** Quarterback in proper throwing position.

Quarterback Drills

Name. Dropback

Purpose. To teach the quarterback to get quickly into proper throwing position.

Organization. The quarterback takes the snap from the center and practices three-, five-, and seven-step drops.

Coaching Points. Have the quarterbacks work on the crossover, backpedal, and rollout drops. Watch for proper footwork, ball-carrying position, and setup.

Name. Set, Pick, and Fire

Purpose. To improve the quarterback's reaction upon setup.

Organization. The quarterback takes a quick drop and sets to deliver the football. Station three or four other players downfield, facing him in a horizontal line spread evenly across the field. Each of these players has an assigned number. The coach calls out one of the numbers. After the quarterback has set his feet, he must quickly reset them in the direction of the designated player and deliver the football to him, using proper throwing mechanics.

Coaching Points. Use an equal number of same-direction and opposite-direction receivers to develop the quarterback's ability to throw to primary and secondary receivers. Watch that upon reset the quarterback gets a solid plant with the back foot.

Name. Shotgun Drill

Purpose. To teach the quarterback to get quickly into proper throwing position. This drill also allows a coach to gauge his quarterback's arm strength.

Organization. The quarterback takes the snap from center at distances of 5, 10, and 15 yards.

Coaching Points. Have the quarterback throw a series of passes—short, medium, deep, quick outs, slants, and hook passes—to receivers on both sides of the center.

Receiving

Running Patterns

When the play is called in the huddle, the receiver is told what pattern to run. This pattern is selected from many options on a pass tree (see figure 7.17). Pass patterns 1, 2, and 3 are reserved for the running backs.

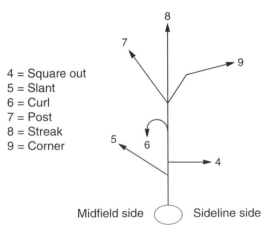

4 = Square out
5 = Slant
6 = Curl
7 = Post
8 = Streak
9 = Corner

Midfield side   Sideline side

■ **Figure 7.17** Pass tree.

The most important thing you should teach a receiver is to *explode* off the line of scrimmage. He should run to the outside shoulder of the defensive back, forcing the defender to turn his shoulders parallel to the line of scrimmage to cover him. Next, the receiver must come under control at the breaking point of the pattern. He then plants his foot, turns his head and shoulders, and reacts to the football.

Catching the Football

The next step in coaching receivers is to teach them how to catch the football. This is a matter of concentration and dedication. The receiver should watch the football into his hands. If the football is thrown high, the receiver should catch it with thumbs together; if it is thrown low, the receiver should catch it with little fingers together. Also, it is important that you teach the receiver to catch the football in his hands and not trap it against his body.

In practices, give receivers the opportunity to catch every type of pass that they will see in games. As a coach, you cannot expect athletes to perform skills in a game that you have not worked on in practice. Instruct receivers to tuck the ball under the arm and protect it after making the catch. Success will help the receivers gain confidence, and touchdowns reinforce that catching the ball is fun.

Receiver Drills

Name. Turn Drill

Purpose. To force the receiver to get into a position to see the ball and concentrate on catching it.

Organization. Two lines of receivers are on each side of the field, with a quarterback throwing to each line. The receiver in each line has his back to the quarterback. The quarterback yells "go" as he passes the ball to the first receiver in line. On the command, the receiver must snap his head around quickly, locate and catch the ball, tuck it in, and turn upfield with it. Have receivers alternate turning the head over each shoulder.

Coaching Points. Work on short, lofted throws initially, with receivers going at three-quarter speed. Increase the speed and length of pass routes as receivers improve.

Name. Concentration Drill

Purpose. To get receivers to focus on the ball and watch it all the way into their hands, even when they know they're going to get hit.

Organization. You'll need several footballs with one-inch numbers painted on each panel and three handheld blocking shields. Three people holding the hand shields line up 3 yards apart, forming an equilateral triangle. Have a receiver run into the middle of the triangle. As the receiver enters it, the quarterback should throw him a high pass. The receiver must jump to catch the pass. When his hands touch the ball, the three players holding shields should jam the receiver with their shields. The receiver must call out the number painted on the ball and hold onto the pass. Figure 7.18 illustrates the Concentration Drill.

Coaching Points. Keep score to determine how many catches and correctly identified numbers receivers have at the end of the drill. Track their improvement throughout the season.

■ **Figure 7.18** Concentration Drill.

Kicking Game

The kicking game is an important part of football. About one-fourth of the game involves kicking, so you definitely need to spend time on it. Three phases of the kicking game that we address in this chapter are the punt, the placekick, and the kickoff.

The Punt

The punt is used on fourth down to turn the ball over to the opponent. The punting team's objective is to give the opponent a less favorable field position. Coach your kickers to follow these guidelines to punt successfully.

- ✔ Line up 10 yards behind the center.
- ✔ Assume a comfortable stance with knees slightly bent and arms extended.
- ✔ When you drop the ball, there should be no movement at the elbows, wrists, or shoulders.
- ✔ Drop the ball perfectly parallel to the ground with the tip turned slightly in.
- ✔ Your foot speed is not as important as making proper contact on the center of the ball.
- ✔ The nonkicking leg should remain in contact with the ground.
- ✔ Allow the kicking leg to extend and follow through after the kick (see figure 7.19).

The key to coaching a punter is to teach him correct technique and then allow him to practice and develop his rhythm. He should strive for consistency in height and distance.

■ **Figure 7.19**   Proper kicking technique for punter.

Punt coverage involves organizing your punt team so that they can protect the punter; cover the punt; and tackle, touch, or pull the flag of the ballcarrier before he can advance the ball upfield. The punter should kick the ball for distance and keep it in the air long enough to give the coverage team time to get downfield and make the tackle, pull the flag, or make the touch. Figure 7.20 shows a common punt coverage team alignment for tackle football. Figure 7.21 shows a common punt coverage team alignment for flag and touch football. In this coverage, the two outside linemen are contain players; they must not let anyone outside them. All other players should always stay in their lanes and let the ball come to them.

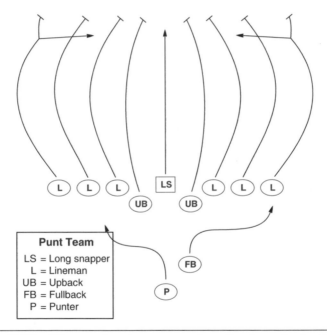

■ **Figure 7.20**   Alignment and coverage of punting team for tackle football.

The Placekick

There are two basic types of placekicking—straight-ahead style (see figure 7.22) and soccer style (see figure 7.23). Both are effective. Have your kickers follow these coaching points, regardless of the kicking style they use.

✔ Emphasize accuracy on every kick.
✔ Avoid overpowering the ball; maintain good timing and rhythm.

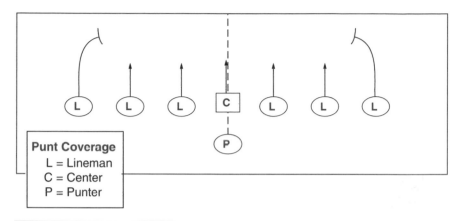

■ **Figure 7.21**   Alignment and coverage of punting team for flag and touch football.

■ **Figure 7.22**   Straight-ahead style of placekicking.

■ **Figure 7.23**   Soccer style of placekicking.

✔ Make proper contact with the ball.
✔ Plant the foot in the same way on each kick.
✔ Hit the ball squarely each time.
✔ Align the body properly on each kick.

Give kickers the opportunity to practice kicking in game-like situations.

The Kickoff

The main difference between the kickoff and the placekick involves the approach phase of the kick. A longer approach run is used on the kickoff, allowing the kicker to build up more speed and momentum before the kick.

The kicker lines up 5 to 10 yards from the football. As he approaches the ball, he must adjust his steps so that he runs through the ball without slowing. The key coaching point on the kickoff is for the kicker to make contact with the ball and work on being consistent. Figure 7.24 shows proper coverage for a kickoff in tackle football. Figure 7.25 shows proper coverage for a kickoff in flag and touch football. The two outside linemen are contain men; they must not let anyone outside them. The safety back should hang back to

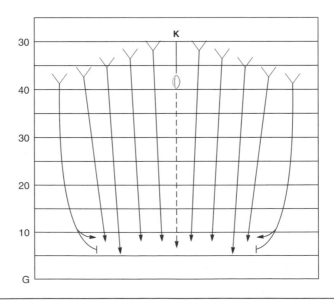

■ **Figure 7.24** Proper coverage for a kickoff in tackle football.

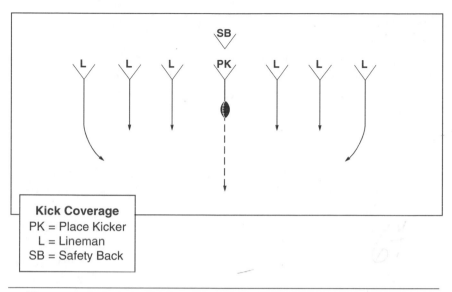

Kick Coverage
PK = Place Kicker
L = Lineman
SB = Safety Back

■ **Figure 7.25**   Proper coverage for a kickoff in flag and touch football.

prevent any long return from becoming a touchdown. All other players should always stay in their lanes and let the ball come to them.

Spend time daily working to improve some phase of your team's kicking game.

DEFENSIVE SKILLS

Playing defense is part instinct, part effort, and part technique. You can't do much about your players' instinct, and most young players love the game, so effort isn't a problem. What a football coach can do is teach and develop players' defensive skills. The rest of this unit will tell you how.

Stance

The proper initial alignment of the body for the defensive player is very important. Teach the defensive linemen, linebackers, and defensive backs the proper stances for their respective positions.

Defensive Linemen

The typical stance for defensive linemen is similar to the offensive lineman's three-point stance (refer to figure 7.1). However, in tackle football some defensive linemen are more comfortable with the outside hand on the ground, creating a four-point stance as shown in figure 7.26. Defensive linemen in flag football use the three-point stance (see figure 7.27). Give your players the following pointers:

- ✔ Placing more weight on the hands enables you to move forward.
- ✔ A stance that is a little wider allows for better balance when you're being blocked.
- ✔ Keep your outside hand (the hand away from the blocker) free to try pass rush techniques and to keep from getting hooked.
- ✔ Keep your body low to the ground and control the line of scrimmage from underneath the opponent's shoulder pads (tackle football).
- ✔ Keep your body low to the ground and use your speed and quickness to get by the blocking backs (flag and touch football).
- ✔ A spin move or a stutter step will help you keep the blocker off balance.

■ **Figure 7.26** Four-point stance for a defensive lineman.

■ **Figure 7.27** Three-point stance for a defensive lineman.

Linebackers

The linebacker should have a good balanced stance, which means that his feet are shoulder-width apart and slightly staggered. Figure 7.28 shows the proper stance for a linebacker. Teach your linebackers the following points:

✔ Bend your knees slightly to ensure low body position.
✔ Poise the arms in front of the body as you get ready to take on a blocker.
✔ Focus your eyes on the man you are to get the key from.
✔ Have one foot slightly forward; step with this foot first as you react to the key and find the football.

■ **Figure 7.28**   Proper stance for a linebacker.

Defensive Backs

Coach the defensive backs to line up with a slightly staggered stance in a relaxed position. Figure 7.29 shows the proper stance for a defensive back. Instruct your players as follows:

✔ Keep your feet slightly staggered, with the outside foot back.
✔ Point the toes straight ahead.
✔ Focus eyes on the man you are to key.
✔ Assume a slightly crouching position with your knees bent a little.
✔ Take a short read step on the snap, and then react to the play.

■ **Figure 7.29**   Proper stance for a defensive back.

■ Stance Drills ■

Name.   Winning From the Start

Purpose.   To teach defensive players the proper presnap position and initial movement.

Organization.   Have your players line up according to their position—defensive linemen, linebackers, and defensive backs—and instruct them to get into their proper stances. Then visually inspect the stances using the guidelines presented in this section to make sure they are correct. Next, have each player move quickly out of his stance to perform his responsibility, so that on the snap count, the defensive linemen step forward, the defensive backs go backward, and the linebackers go forward, laterally, or backward. Watch to make sure players do not take false steps and that they maintain a good hitting position throughout their movement.

Coaching Points.   Vary quick and long counts to keep players from anticipating the snap. Have them hurry back into position each time and have them try different positions during the drill.

Tackling

If you want to have a good defensive team, you must teach your defensive players to tackle. Players who are just beginning to learn the game may only be able to get into a position to grab the runner and pull him down, but as the players grow and progress, it is important that you teach them the proper techniques of tackling.

The tackler should always be in the proper hitting position and have a target to focus on in making the tackle (this is usually the area of the runner's belt buckle). If the tackler focuses on this target, his opponent will not be able to fake him out with a fancy shoulder move. The three basic tackles that your players will be using are the head-on tackle, the angle tackle, and the open-field tackle. Here are some coaching points for each type.

Head-On Tackle

Defensive players use the head-on tackle when they line up straight across from the offensive runner coming toward them.

The tackler should first make sure he is in a good hitting position and is ready to make the tackle. Emphasize the following points to your tacklers:

✔ Make sure that you are under control so as not to overrun the ballcarrier or dive and miss the tackle.

✔ Maintain a wide, balanced stance; keep the feet moving with choppy steps.

✔ Extend your arms and head in front of your body.

✔ Keep your head up, your back arched, and your knees slightly bent.

✔ Slide your head to the outside just before making contact.

✔ Drive your shoulder into the runner's stomach region as you thrust your hips through.

✔ With your arms, grasp behind the legs of the ballcarrier and pull him toward you.

✔ Lift and pull the ballcarrier toward you as you take him off his feet.

Figure 7.30 shows proper tackling technique. This is the tackle technique that you should teach your young athletes.

■ **Figure 7.30**   Proper tackling technique.

Angle Tackle

This tackle is necessary when the ballcarrier runs a wide play or gets close to the sideline. Coach your tacklers using these guidelines:

- ✔ Keep under control and be ready to move in any direction.
- ✔ Maintain a good balanced stance in a good hitting position.
- ✔ Drive your head in front of the ballcarrier's number, across the line of his run.
- ✔ Drive your shoulder upward on the runner at about waist level.
- ✔ With your arms, grasp the runner behind the legs and lift him off the ground.
- ✔ Arch your back to lift and drive through the ballcarrier.
- ✔ Keep the feet moving with short, choppy steps as you finish the tackle.

Open-Field Tackle

After the runner has cleared the line of scrimmage or when a receiver has caught the football and has just one man to beat, defensive players must make an open-field tackle. Coach your players that in the open field the most important thing to do is to get hold of the opponent and pull him to the ground. Stress these coaching points:

- ✔ Keep under control with your legs bent.
- ✔ Use the sideline to your advantage, penning in or getting an angle on the runner.
- ✔ Your number one priority is to grasp the runner.
- ✔ Once you have a hold on the runner, help should soon arrive. But, if possible, try to drive the ballcarrier out of bounds or pull him to the turf.
- ✔ Don't worry about driving through the man or delivering a hard blow. Your sole responsibility is to get hold of the player and prevent the score.

■ Tackling Drills ■

Name.   Form Tackling Drill

Purpose.   To teach players the basic tackling techniques.

Organization.   Form two lines of players with the leaders of each line facing each other. One will be the ballcarrier and the other the defensive player. The ballcarrier runs straight at the defensive player. The defensive player must first get into a position to tackle the ballcarrier and then make the tackle. The next players in line then continue the drill, and so on.

Coaching Points.   Have players walk through the drill to start. As their technique improves, gradually increase the speed and intensity of the drill. Stand near and to the side of the point of contact and make corrections according to the techniques described in the tackling section.

Name.   Sideline Tackling or Touching Drill

Purpose.   To teach the players to use the sideline to their advantage and judge the angle to make the tackle or touch.

Organization.   The ballcarrier lines up behind the quarterback on the hash mark, takes the pitch, and runs a sweep toward the sideline. The defensive player is 5 yards in front of the center, and he runs on an angle to intersect the ballcarrier before he can get outside and down the sideline. The defensive man should execute the angle tackle or touch as described in the tackling and touch sections (see figure 7.31).

Coaching Points.   Match up players of similar size and speed. Give defenders enough repetitions that they become proficient at making this tackle or touch.

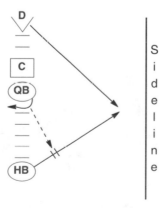

■ **Figure 7.31**   Sideline Tackling or Touching Drill.

Pulling the Flag or Touching

If you want to have a good defensive team in flag football, you must teach your defensive players to pull flags. In touch football, you must coach your players on the proper techniques of tagging a player. Players who learn the correct fundamentals of flag pulling and touching early can more easily develop skills as they get older.

Head-On Flag Pull or Touch

The head-on flag pull or touch is used when the defensive player is lined up straight across from the offensive runner coming toward him. Keep low and center your attention on his waist. Figure 7.32 illustrates proper flag pulling technique. Figure 7.33 illustrates proper touching technique. Emphasize the following points to your flag pullers or touchers:

- ✔ Make sure that you are under control so as not to overrun the ballcarrier or dive and miss the flag pull or touch.
- ✔ Maintain a wide balanced stance; keep the feet moving with choppy steps.
- ✔ Extend your arms and head in front of your body.
- ✔ Keep your head up, your back arched, and your knees slightly bent.
- ✔ Slide your body to one side to avoid contact and reach for the flag or touch the runner with two hands.

■ **Figure 7.32** Proper flag-pulling technique.

■ **Figure 7.33**   Proper touching technique.

Angle Flag Pull or Touch

This flag pull or touch is necessary when the ballcarrier runs a wide play or gets close to the sideline. Coach your defensive players using these guidelines:

- ✔ Keep under control and be ready to move in any direction.
- ✔ Maintain a good balanced stance and stay on your feet with your head up.
- ✔ Reach for the flag or touch the runner with your body under control, head up, eyes focused on the ballcarrier's waist or numbers.
- ✔ Stay relaxed as you pull the flag or touch the ballcarrier.

Open-Field Flag Pull or Touch

After the runner has cleared the line of scrimmage or when a receiver has caught the football and has just one man to beat, the defender must use the open-field flag pull or touch. Coach your players that in the open field the most important thing to do is get close enough to the ballcarrier that they can pull the flag or touch him. Stress these coaching points:

✔ Keep under control with your legs bent.
✔ Keep your feet moving, head up, and arms out away from your body.
✔ Use the sideline to your advantage, penning in or getting an angle on the runner.
✔ Your sole responsibility is to prevent the score by pulling the flag or touching the runner.

■ Flag-Pulling and Touching Drills ■

Name. Form Flag-Pulling and Touching Drill

Purpose. To teach players basic flag-pulling and touching techniques.

Organization. Have one player stand facing the rest of the team, which is lined up in a single file. Position the single player between two cones 5 to 7 yards apart. Have the other players, each in turn, run at the defending player, who will attempt to pull their flags or touch. This drill is illustrated in figure 7.34.

Coaching Points. Have players walk through the drill to start. As their technique improves, gradually increase the speed and intensity of the drill. Stand near and to the side of the point of contact and make corrections according to the techniques described in the flag-pulling and touching sections.

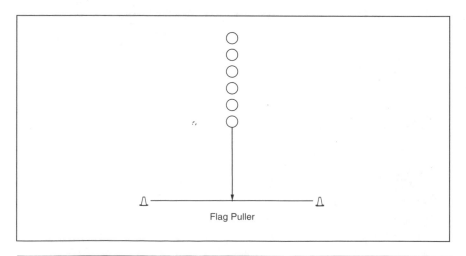

Flag Puller

■ **Figure 7.34** Form Flag-Pulling and Touching Drill.

Name.   Sideline Flag Pulling

Purpose.   To teach the players to use the sideline to their advantage and judge the angle to make the flag pull.

Organization.   The ballcarrier lines up behind the quarterback on the hash mark, takes the pitch, and runs a sweep toward the sideline. The defensive player is 5 yards in front of the center, and he runs on an angle to intersect the ballcarrier before he can get outside and down the sideline. The defensive man should execute the angle flag pull as described in the tackling section.

Coaching Points.   Match up players of similar size and speed. Give defenders enough repetitions that they become proficient at making this flag pull.

Rushing the Passer

To improve the pass rush of the defensive linemen, you can teach them the following techniques.

Bull Rush

A bull rush occurs when the defensive man gets control of the offensive blocker by locking his arms in the offensive blocker's armpits, and, with the leverage provided by locking his elbows, lifts the offensive lineman up, forcing him back into the quarterback. This type of rush requires good arm and hand strength.

Swim Technique

The defender employs this technique by driving hard for the blocker's outside shoulder, forcing him to square up and set himself for the rush (see figure 7.35). When the blocker begins to square up and set, the defender brings his outside arm up and hits the opponent on the side of the shoulder in an attempt to knock him off balance. Next, the pass rusher brings his inside arm over the top of the blocker's outside shoulder in a swimming motion. Once the inside arm is over the blocker, the defender pushes off and moves toward the quarterback. Note that the swim motion and the pushoff must be one continuous movement.

■ **Figure 7.35** Swim technique.

Undercut Technique

With the undercut technique, the defender attacks the blocker low and hard. As he closes toward the offensive player, he executes a forearm blow with his inside arm to the blocker's inside shoulder. The purpose of this maneuver is to turn the blocker's shoulders toward the undercut side. As the blocker's shoulder turns, the defender steps inside with his outside foot and ducks under the blocker, continuing on to the quarterback. The player must coordinate the forearm shiver and undercut as one continuous movement.

■ Pass Rush Drills ■

Name.   Pass Rush Technique

Purpose.   To teach techniques for rushing the passer.

Organization.   Position your defensive lineman on an imaginary line of scrimmage facing an offensive lineman or blocking back. Instruct the offensive lineman or blocking back to set up in a pass protection position. Then instruct the defensive lineman to walk through the bull rush, swim, and undercut techniques to get to the quarterback.

Coaching Points.   Observe and make corrections, stopping the action whenever necessary. When players have mastered the basic techniques, have them progress to a one-on-one drill against the offensive line to see how well they employ the techniques in a game-like situation.

Covering Receivers

The defense must be able to cover the receivers to stop the offense from moving the ball through the air. Spend time training your players to defend the pass. Following are some of the necessary skills.

Proper Alignment

The defensive corners should line up 5 to 7 yards off the wide receivers. The safeties should line up 8 to 12 yards deep off the tight end or slot receiver. If you are playing only one safety, he should line up deep in the middle of the field.

Backpedal

Instruct your players to bend at the waist with a forward body lean. The backpedal should start with a step backward with the back foot and a push off the front foot. As the player backpedals he should reach back with each step and pull his body over his feet. His arms should move in a normal, relaxed running fashion. The player should be under control so that when the receiver makes his break to catch the ball, the defensive man is ready to drive on him.

Pass Coverage

The basic coverage in tackle football is man-to-man. This means that a defensive player is assigned to each offensive receiver wherever he goes. Figure 7.36 shows an example of man-to-man coverage in tackle football. Figure 7.37 shows an example of man-to-man coverage in flag and touch football. Use the following guidelines in teaching your players how to cover receivers:

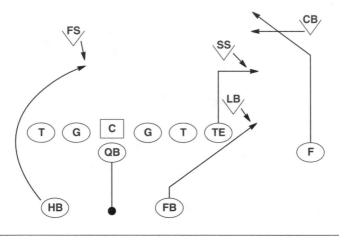

■ **Figure 7.36** Man-to-man coverage in tackle football.

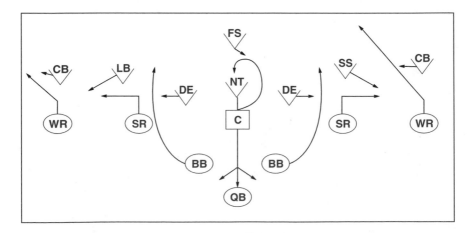

■ **Figure 7.37** Man-to-man coverage in flag and touch football.

✔ Keep your eyes focused primarily on the receiver you are covering (at his belt region).
✔ Maintain a 3- to 4-yard cushion between you and the receiver.
✔ Never turn your back on the receiver.
✔ Once the ball is in the air, play it aggressively.

Zone Coverage

In flag and touch football, teams use zone coverage extensively because of the speed of the game and because flag and touch is 90 percent passing. A relatively inexperienced player can more easily learn the game and its techniques by playing zone rather than man-to-man. Figures 7.38 and 7.39 show two different zone coverages. Use the following guidelines in teaching your players how to play a zone and cover receivers:

✔ Keep your eyes open and your head up to be alert for players running into your zone.
✔ Maintain a 3- or 4-yard cushion between you and the receiver.
✔ Never turn your back on the receiver.
✔ Once the ball is in the air, play it aggressively.

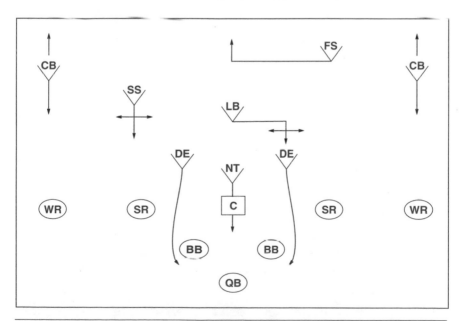

■ **Figure 7.38** Zone coverage: (3-2) 3 deep, 2 short, 3 rush.

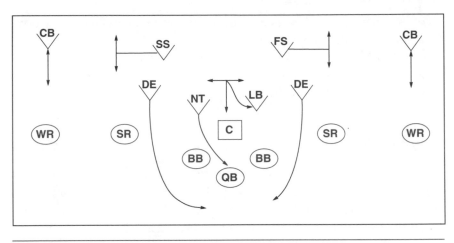

■ **Figure 7.39** Zone coverage: (4-across) 4 deep, 4-man line.

In a 4-across (figure 7.39) the linebacker lines up on the line of scrimmage to fake a blitz, then drops off and covers the center or the middle short zone.

Covering Receiver Drills

Name. Backpedal Drill

Purpose. To teach players the proper fundamentals of executing the backpedal.

Organization. The defensive player faces the coach. As you raise the ball, he begins his backpedal. After he has backpedaled about 10 yards, throw a catchable pass to the right or left of the defensive man.

Coaching Points. Make sure that the defensive man follows the techniques discussed in the section on covering receivers. Emphasize that defenders must drive toward the football when they see its direction and flight.

Name. Square Drill

Purpose. To help players develop the ability to break squarely from a backpedal.

Organization. The defensive player aligns near the hash mark. As you raise the ball, the defender backpedals 5 to 7 yards, and you move the ball to the player's right. The player turns and breaks squarely to his right, sprinting hard 5 yards and then coasting 5 yards (see figure 7.40). Two to four players can perform the drill in the same box.

Coaching Points. Make sure that players make a proper plant step when changing direction; try to correct players who make false steps.

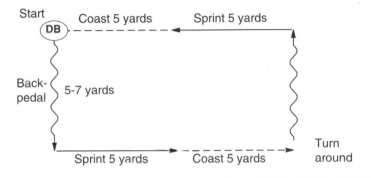

■ **Figure 7.40** Square Drill.

Unit 8

How Do I Get My Players to Play as a Team?

To be a successful coach, you must develop a football coaching philosophy. We talked about your coaching outlook in unit 2. But a football coaching philosophy is more specific to the sport—what you consider most important and what you emphasize to players when teaching the Xs and Os.

After you've developed a philosophy, you'll need to establish strategies that your players can learn and implement in a game situation. You'll set offensive goals and decide what kind of offense you want to employ to move the football. You'll also set defensive goals and decide what defense you'll run. You must also determine your approach on special teams and the amount of time you'll spend to develop these skills.

Offensive Goals

The objectives you set must be realistic and important—not just to you, but to your players. If your team is incapable of reaching the goals, or is not interested in achieving them, then they serve little purpose.

Scoring is the obvious objective when a football team is on offense. But scoring is an outcome produced by the team's ability to

- execute consistently,
- move the football, and
- maintain possession.

Execute Consistently

To execute consistently, you must run the same plays throughout the season and work on them continually. Select a simple offense and teach it well. A few well-executed plays can give even the best opponents all they can handle. If your offense has too many plays, chances are your team, not your opponent, will be confused.

Consistent execution stems from your athletes' understanding the plays and practicing them repeatedly. Every player must know what is expected of him for each running play. Practicing these plays against the defense that you expect opponents to play will help your players visualize the way they should run each play. If your players know that a team goal is consistent execution, they'll be more eager to perform the plays as often as necessary to make them work in a game.

Approach your team's passing game the same way. Teach your receivers the proper patterns to run and your quarterback the proper depth to drop to throw the football. Your players need to practice running the pattern several times before they'll feel confident that it will work. You might run one pattern as many as 30 times in practice before you use it in a game.

Develop a game plan early in the week and then simplify it so that on game day you have only five running plays, five pass patterns, and two goal line plays. By using a limited number of plays each week and giving the players enough repetitions to eliminate mistakes, you'll help your team execute consistently

Know the SCORE

Here is a positive slogan that reminds you and your players that doing the basics well is the key to success:

S	Simple as you can make it.
C	Complete instructions for each player.
O	One player executing poorly makes the whole team suffer.
R	Repeat many times.
E	Every player is involved.

Move the Football

The object of offensive football is to move down the field and score, by either throwing the ball or running it. Running basic plays against the defense you anticipate seeing is the best way to prepare your team to move the football in a game.

The offensive team must believe they can march the football down the field regardless of the team they're playing or the defense they're facing. Use your play selection to expose a defense's weakness and play to the strength of your offense.

Maintain Possession

The offense should be aware that when they control the football, the opponent cannot score. To keep control, the offense must consistently produce first downs and keep the clock running. An effective running game combined with a good short passing game is hard to stop. Four yards a crack on running plays and high-percentage, 5- to 10-yard passes can keep the chains moving steadily toward the opponent's goal line.

Maintaining possession is especially important when your team has a narrow lead at the end of a game. The other team can't score if it doesn't get the ball.

Score

The touchdown is the primary objective and the field goal a secondary objective on an offensive drive. Passing may get you to the goal line faster, but a long march to the goal by way of the running game can take the heart out of the other team's defense. And there's nothing like a touchdown or a field goal to get your team fired up. Your team will be more excited and execute with more intensity if they experience the rewards of their efforts. Scoring gives the players confidence and reinforces the system you are using to coach.

Offensive Strategies

A coach builds a successful offense by combining an effective offensive system with a well-conceived game plan. The offensive system should have both a solid running game and an effective passing attack.

Running Game

In flag and touch football, the running game is secondary because blocking is restricted and the number of linemen is limited. Figure 8.1 shows a few plays that will help you open up a defense and make them respect the run instead of just sitting back waiting for you to pass. The rules of flag and touch football do not permit double teams or two-on-one blocking.

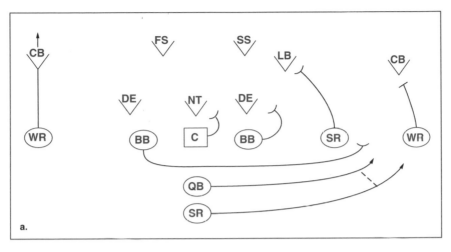

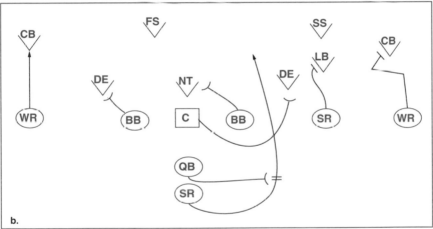

■ **Figure 8.1**   Two schemes for running plays in flag and touch football: (a) end sweep and (b) up the middle.

In tackle football, you must develop an effective running game. The most important step is to design plays in which the blocking and backfield action work together. The backfield action on any play must be designed to put the running back at the point of attack just as the hole is opening. Three types of blocks can help accomplish this: fast or quick blocking on straight-ahead plays, fold blocking on slower-hitting plays, and power blocking on sweeps. Figure 8.2 shows examples of the three types of blocking.

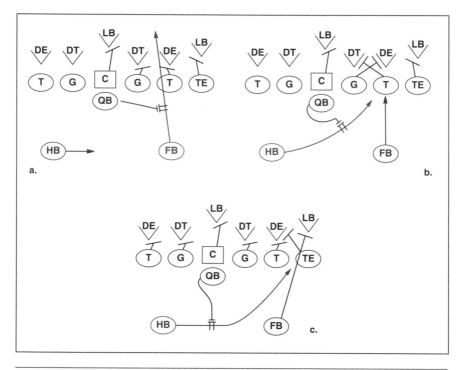

■ **Figure 8.2** Three basic schemes for running plays in tackle football: (a) straight man-for-man block, (b) fold blocking, and (c) power blocking (double team).

You should also set up the running game so that it is effective and easy to communicate. The simplest way to communicate running plays is to number each hole and back. Figure 8.3 shows how to do this in tackle football. The running back runs the ball into the hole that is called. For example, play 32 means that the number 3 back runs the ball through the number 2 hole. Figure 8.4 shows a similar numbering system for flag and touch football.

In developing a running game, you should consider different series of plays that can all be successful. All series should include built-in dimension—that part of a given series that provides for variation of backfield movement. Dimension makes it difficult for the defense to determine the point of attack when the ball is snapped. This forces the defense to respect your entire attack. An example of a series is a dive 30 and a trap 30. These both involve the number 3 back running through the hole right in the center of the line, but the back gets there by different actions and the blocking is different.

The running game should give you the opportunity to run the football in every offensive hole. By incorporating series of plays, you'll be able to run the various holes in more than one way. The game plan, however, should include only four or five running plays chosen from the total series of plays. These are the plays you will perfect for a given opponent.

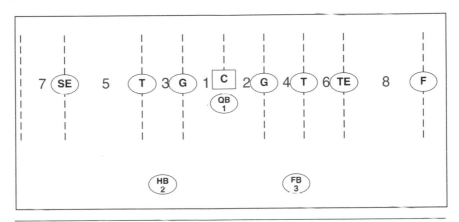

■ **Figure 8.3**   Numbering of holes and backs for tackle football.

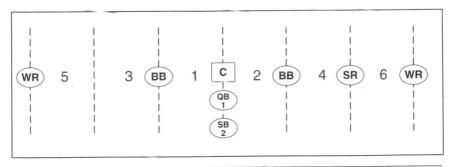

■ **Figure 8.4**   Numbering of holes and backs for flag and touch football.

Successful football teams use runs that are effective against the opponent they are playing. For example, if the defense is coming across the line of scrimmage very hard, you would use the trap series. Against a hard-charging defense, it is easier for an offensive lineman to get an angle if a trap is called. Sometimes the defender will take himself out of (overrun) the play; other times he can be blocked from the side. Against a reading defense, the dive and sweep would be effective. If the defense stacks the line of scrimmage, you may be better off throwing the ball.

The running backs are an integral part of a good running offense. Coach them to gain yardage on every play. They should be competitive and have the desire to be successful. A running back who is hard to tackle, who keeps his feet driving, and who is at times his own blocker will make you and your team winners.

Passing Game

The forward pass is a potent way to gain yardage and score points. Throwing the football helps develop individual players, forces the defense to defend the whole field, gains yardage on offense, and appeals to the crowd.

If you plan to pass the football, you must do a good job of drilling the quarterbacks and receivers in the basic skills covered in unit 7. Keep the passing attack simple so that the quarterbacks and receivers know what to do. Timing is important to the success of a passing attack, so you must allow time in practice for players to perform many repetitions of the basic patterns.

The passing game starts with a pass tree (see figure 7.17). These are patterns that the receivers run to get open to catch the football. The quarterback drops straight back (as described on pages 115-116) and throws the football to the open receiver.

Different pass patterns may be helpful in different situations. When the defensive man retreats too fast, use the curl pattern. The receiver drives deep and then curls back to the football (see figure 8.5a). The square out pattern is very successful when the defensive man is playing off the receiver (see figure 8.5b). The receiver runs downfield 10 yards and then cuts sharply to the sideline, catching the ball just before he steps out of bounds. A crossing pattern is effective against man-to-man coverage. Figure 8.5c shows two receivers crossing downfield. The defensive man is screened off on the crossing action, and one of the receivers usually comes open. Use the last pattern, the streak, if the defensive back is playing tight on a receiver with speed. The receiver shows a curl move, then breaks to the outside and sprints down the sideline (see figure 8.5d).

The passing game takes time to develop, and you must be patient to bring the separate parts of this offense together. The next two drills should help.

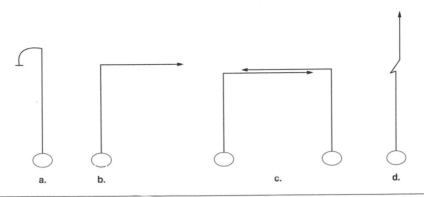

■ Figure 8.5 Pass patterns: (a) curl, (b) square out, (c) crossing, and (d) streak.

▣ Offensive Team Drills ▣

Name. Pass Skeleton

Purpose. To develop the quarterback's passing skills and give the receivers a chance to run their patterns against a preparation defense.

Organization. The skeleton offensive group (quarterback, three receivers, and two running backs for tackle football; quarterback, two wide receivers, two slot receivers, and center for flag and touch football) lines up on the line of scrimmage and runs pass patterns against the linebackers and defensive backs (figure 8.6). The defense is told what defense to run while the offensive group works on their pass play execution.

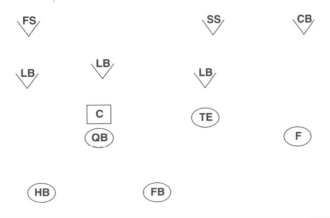

■ Figure 8.6 Pass Skeleton Drill for tackle football.

Coaching Points. Mix in some play-action passes emphasizing good fakes by the quarterback and running backs. Encourage receivers to run crisp routes, using feints and bursts to elude the coverage. Also, try to determine what type and length of passes the quarterback can complete consistently.

Name. Team Offense

Purpose. To run all the offensive runs and passes against a defensive unit.

Organization. The plays that you are planning to run in the game are called in the huddle and then run against a team of defenders who react to the football but let the offense block them. The backs and receivers go at full speed.

Coaching Points. Look for offensive linemen to blow off the line of scrimmage and get a jump on the defense. Emphasize quickness and execution at the skill positions.

Defensive Goals

Every defense has a purpose. You can design your defense to either blitz, penetrate, pursue, contain, or perform any number of tactics to disrupt or stop the offense. Your defensive approach should reflect the talents of your players. Your basic defensive alignment must capitalize on their strengths and compensate for their weaknesses.

For example, if you have a somewhat big, slow team, use more linemen on the line of scrimmage and try to control and contain the offense. If you have a small, quick team, use more linebackers and do more blitzing to take advantage of their quickness. Once you have determined your style of defense, stay with it.

The three most important goals a defense can strive to accomplish are

- to prevent the easy touchdown,
- to get possession of the ball, and
- to score.

Prevent the Easy Touchdown

Although the obvious objective of defensive football is to keep the opposition from scoring, a more functional objective of defensive play is to prevent the opposition from scoring the easy touchdown with a long pass or a long run. Make your opponent earn every point it scores by having a defense that challenges every yard. Praise players for preventing first downs and stopping the opponent's drives downfield.

Get Possession of the Ball

In tackle football, the defensive team may gain possession of the ball by holding the opponent to less than 10 yards on four downs, forcing a punt, intercepting a pass, recovering a fumble, or blocking a punt. Turnovers can also motivate a defense when it is having trouble stopping an opponent.

In flag and touch football, the defensive team may gain possession of the ball by preventing the opponent from gaining the next zone line to gain on four downs, forcing a punt, intercepting a pass, recovering a fumble that has not yet hit the ground, or blocking a punt on a live-rush punt situation

Score

In tackle football, the defense can score by returning a punt or an intercepted pass, by advancing a blocked punt, by recovering a fumble in the end zone, by advancing any fumbled ball for a score, or by tackling the offensive player in his end zone for a safety.

In flag and touch football, the defense can score by returning a punt or an intercepted pass, by blocking a punt in the end zone for a safety on a live-rush punt, or by recovering a fumble in the end zone before it hits the ground. Remember that all fumbles in flag and touch football are dead at the spot to avoid pileups and subsequent injuries. The defense can also score by pulling the flag or touching the offensive player in his end zone for a safety.

Defensive Strategies

You should have a plan for every situation your defense faces. In developing that plan, remember to include tactics that attack the offense and make things happen. In addition, your defensive scheme must include options to contain the offense in long-yardage situations.

Attacking Defense

Use the following information to coach your defensive team to attack any running or passing game.

Alignments

If the offense is moving the ball, the defense must adjust alignment during the game to slow them down. For example, if the opponent is running the ball up the middle at your linebackers, switch to a defense that puts a defensive lineman in the middle.

Proper Keys

A defensive skill that is more important at advanced levels is the ability to "read" what the offense is going to do before the ball is snapped. The obvious advantage to doing this is that your defenders will be able to anticipate the play and stop it. If you try to teach your players how to read the offense, keep the reads few and simple.

The most basic read is made by "keying" on an opponent's formation, tendencies in play selection, or individual player cues. For example, a defensive back may key on the offensive tackle or blocking back (flag and touch football) on his side of the field. If he sees the lineman or blocking back set up to pass protect, he can assume it's a pass play and focus on covering his receiver. If the defensive back sees the lineman or blocking back drive block, he can anticipate a running play and move into position to stop the ballcarrier.

Flexibility

By having a knowledge of football and learning as much as you can about your defense's strengths and weaknesses, you will be able to make the proper adjustments during the game. The coach must prepare the defense to cover various formations and series of plays. For example, if you are running a three-deep secondary and the offense is passing the ball, you may go to the four-deep secondary.

If the offense gives you an unusual formation, your defensive players must know how to adjust. The offense's position on the field, the score, the time left in the game, and the type of offense your team is facing are all factors that influence the defense that you should run.

As the coach, you might consider limiting the defense according to the skill level of your team. It is more effective to run a few defenses well than to run many defenses poorly.

The skills that we talked about in unit 7 are good guidelines to incorporate into the total picture of a team defense. Team defense involves a group of players performing their individual techniques for the good of the team. Get the right players at the point of attack at the right time, and your team will be successful.

Defense Must Be Fun

Defensive football players are the aggressive kids who love to run and make contact. If you encourage emotion in defensive players, they will become excited when they make a tackle, touch, or flag pull, recover a fumble, or intercept a pass. This excitement adds to team unity, and the players will perform at a higher level.

In tackle football, it is important to encourage team tackling (where more than one person tackles the ballcarrier). This motivates defensive players to swarm to the ballcarrier and adds to team spirit. Stress hard work in an attempt to gain success, but make sure you add fun to the game.

Pressure Defense

The pressure defense is designed to force the offensive team into making mistakes. An example of this is when the defense forces the quarterback to throw the football before he is ready. Teach your defensive players the following points:

- ✔ A pressure defense uses a man-to-man pass coverage and tries to bump the receiver as he starts to run his pattern.
- ✔ The linebackers attack the line of scrimmage on the snap, trying to disrupt the offensive players' blocking schemes.

✔ In tackle football, the defensive alignment employs eight men within 5 yards of the line of scrimmage who can rush.
✔ In flag and touch football, the defensive alignment employs four men within 5 yards of the line of scrimmage who can rush.
✔ Defensive players can jump up into the line of scrimmage and then retreat. They can loop on their pass rush. They can rush two players through the same defensive hole to confuse the offense.

The pressure defense is a good strategy to use if you have confidence in your players' abilities and techniques. This is important because in this defense your defensive backs are isolated one-on-one with their receivers with no help from the safety.

The pressure defense changes the tempo of the game, preventing the opponent from retaining possession of the football and driving down the field. The pressure defense is a good change-up; use it when the offense is not expecting it. If you find a blitz that gives the offense trouble or that they cannot pick up, keep using it until they make the proper adjustment. Figure 8.7 shows a sample alignment for a pressure defense in tackle football. Figure 8.8 shows a sample alignment for flag and touch football.

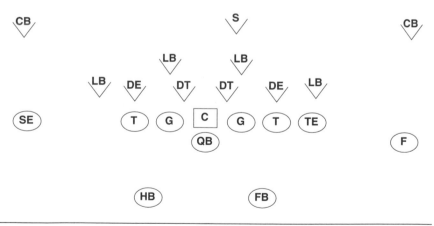

■ **Figure 8.7** Alignment for a pressure defense in tackle football.

Contain Defense

The contain defense plays a little softer than the pressure defense and tries to keep the offense from getting outside or getting deep. The defensive ends play for position to prevent ballcarriers from

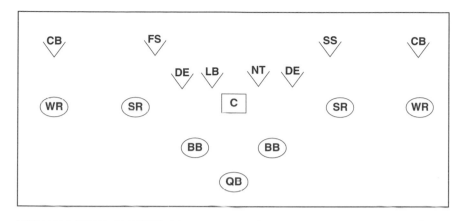

■ **Figure 8.8** Alignment for a pressure defense in flag and touch football.

getting outside them. After the defensive player reads his key, he first controls the gap or area of the field that he is responsible for and then reacts to the football. The defensive backs employ a zone coverage on passes to ensure that the receivers do not get behind them.

This type of defense requires disciplined players who carry out their assignments. It is effective in long-yardage situations just before the half and at the end of the game to ensure a victory.

Coaching is important to the success of a contain defense. The defensive players must recognize formations, types of running plays, and types of passes and must adjust to stop the play. Figure 8.9 shows a basic alignment for a contain defense in tackle football. Figure 8.10 shows a basic alignment for a contain defense in flag and touch football.

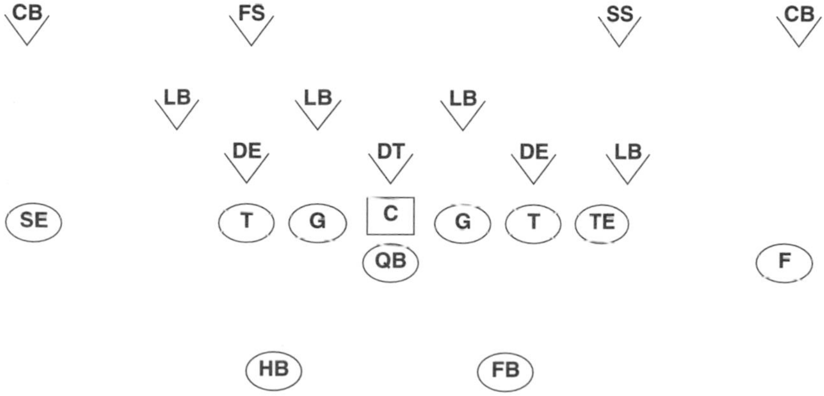

■ **Figure 8.9** Alignment for a contain defense in tackle football.

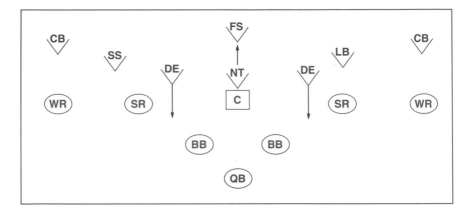

■ **Figure 8.10** Alignment for a contain defense in flag and touch football.

Defense Team Drills

Name. Defensive Coverage

Purpose. To give the defensive backs and linebackers the opportunity to recognize pass routes and cover receivers.

Organization. The skeleton offensive group runs your next opponent's patterns, which the coach has drawn on cards. The quarterback drops to the proper depth, and the receivers run the patterns that the opponent does. When the quarterback throws the ball to one of the receivers, the defensive players try to cover the pattern and intercept the ball (see figures 8.11 and 8.12). This drill gives the defensive players a chance to work against the pass patterns they will see in the next game and the opportunity to work on their execution to stop the pass.

Coaching Points. Emphasize the use of technique and position as dictated by the coverage called. Award a point to the offense for completing a pass and a point to the defense for incomplete or intercepted passes. Play to 10 points.

Name. Seven-on-Seven

Purpose. To allow the defensive line and linebackers to defend runs the opponent may use.

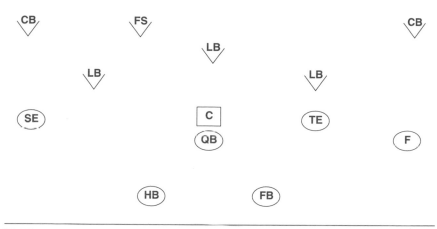

■ **Figure 8.11**   Defensive Coverage Drill for tackle football.

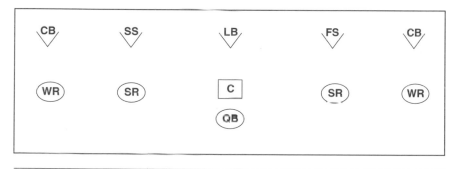

■ **Figure 8.12**   Defensive Coverage Drill for flag and touch football.

Organization.   An offensive team runs the offense from cards showing running plays that the opponent may use in the upcoming game. They block using the opponent's schemes to give the defense the opportunity to read the blocking, see the backfield action, and react to the plays.

Coaching Points.   Watch for accurate alignment, proper use of individual techniques, and sound team execution of the called defense.

Special Teams

The special teams play an integral part in football. Special-team players need to feel that their contribution to the game is important. You can accomplish this by setting goals for the special teams and by developing a successful strategy.

Goals for Special Teams

The main goal of the special teams is to perform their duties in such a way that they help the team win. You may want to consider some specific goals with your team:

- Know and adhere to the six don'ts:
  - ✔ Don't be offside.
  - ✔ Don't rough the kicker.
  - ✔ Don't clip.
  - ✔ Don't block below the waist.
  - ✔ Don't make mistakes.
  - ✔ Don't commit penalties that give the ball back to the offense or give them good field position.
- Win the battle of field position (on a kickoff, keep the opponent inside its 30-yard line). Good kicking and good coverage will accomplish this.
- Eliminate bad snaps.
- Make the big play (turnover, blocked kicks, etc.).

Strategies for Special Teams

A simple, basic plan will win the kicking game if the team executes flawlessly and with full effort. The kicking unit's primary objective is to execute the basic elements of the kicking game without making any big mistakes. Its second objective is to attack an opponent's weakness or exploit a situation when it arises.

The goal of special teams is to execute the basics. The punt coverage team must make sure the ball is kicked before they cover. The

Kicking Game Rules

A player signals a fair catch by extending his arm above his head and waving it from side to side. The receiving player cannot hit or be hit after a fair catch.

The kicking team may down the football after the ball has hit the ground.

No one on either team can block below the waist.

No player on the receiving team may touch the kicker unless the receiving team has blocked it and the kicker runs with the ball.

A field goal is a scrimmage kick and uses the same rules as the punt.

Always be alert for a fake punt or fake field goal attempt.

On a kickoff, after the ball has traveled 10 yards it is a free ball and either team can recover it (only in tackle football).

field goal team must make sure the kick is not blocked before they cover. Also, any time there is a return, the return team must avoid being the victim of a fake play by making sure that the other team has actually put the ball in the air.

By setting goals and developing a sound strategy, you can help make the kicking game a positive part of your football team.

In flag and touch football, you may request a no-rush situation on a punt by asking the referee for "protection." This means that no one on either team may move until the ball is kicked. This rule is for safety reasons and lets teams that are weak in the punting game get off a good punt and develop their coverage teams.

Scrimmages

Scrimmages simulate game situations. There are three types: full-scale scrimmage, controlled scrimmage, and pass scrimmage.

Full-Scale Scrimmage

The full-scale scrimmage is much like a game. Start with a kickoff, punt on fourth down, and keep score. This type of practice activity prepares the offense and defense for competition. However, be cautioned. In tackle football, any time you use tackling and hitting, you risk injury. If you use the full-scale scrimmage, don't do it on a regular basis.

Controlled Scrimmage

In both tackle football and flag and touch football, the controlled scrimmage includes some restrictions. In tackle football, the line blocking is live, but the running backs do not get tackled and the quarterbacks and receivers do not get hit. This type of scrimmage helps the team's timing without the risk of injury to key people. In flag and touch football, the blocking is at half speed to avoid bumps and bruises.

You can use the controlled scrimmage on a regular basis. You may want to emphasize offense for half the scrimmage and defense for the other half. This allows you to use your top players on both offense and defense.

Pass Scrimmage

The pass scrimmage emphasizes passing. In tackle football, the line is still live in the pass scrimmage, but the quarterback and the receivers are not tackled. The pass scrimmage helps the passing attack with timing and gives the defense the opportunity to cover the pass. Use this type of scrimmage on a regular basis because the risk of injury is low and it gives your team a great opportunity to improve its passing attack and pass defense. This type of scrimmage is great for flag and touch football because passing is about 90 percent of the game.

Your players will improve the skills and techniques you teach them only if they practice them at full speed in a game-like situation. For this reason scrimmages are useful in getting your football team ready to play an opponent.

Putting It All Together

Understanding the game, teaching skills, developing a strategy, and formulating a game plan can help make your coaching career successful. However, just because you have taught your players how to block, how to tackle or flag pull or touch, and how to run and pass the football doesn't mean they will always perform these skills successfully in games. Their opponents will have more than a little to say about that.

Coaching Youth Football will help you teach the fundamentals of the game to your players. With the solid foundation you've gained through this book, you should be prepared to move on to teaching your players offensive and defensive football strategies. If you do a good job of teaching, your players will be hooked on football for the rest of their lives. The American Sport Education Program has the courses and resources you need to tackle the job.

Appendix A

Sample Season Plan for Beginning Football Players

Goal: To help players learn and practice the skills and tactics needed to play football games successfully.

T(#) = Initial teaching time (minutes)

* = Techniques or tactics practiced during drills and activities

P(#) = Practice and review time (minutes)

Activity	Practice Sessions					
	1	2	3	4	5	6
Warm-Up	T(10)	T(10)	P(10)	P(10)	P(10)	P(10)
Cool-Down	T(5)	P(5)	P(5)	P(5)	P(5)	P(5)
Evaluation	(5)	(5)	(5)	(5)	(5)	(5)
Stance	T(10)	T(5)	P(5)	*	*	*
Blocking (Offensive linemen, receivers, and running backs)						
Drive	T(10)	P(5)	P(5)		P(10)	*
Downfield				T(5)	P(5)	*
Pass		T(10)	P(5)	P(10)		P(10)
Drills	P(5)	P(10)	P(10)	P(5)	P(10)	P(10)
Running (Some activities for all, others position-specific)						
Form	T(5)	*		*		*
Starts	T(5)	*	*	*	*	*
Drills	P(5)	P(10)	P(15)	P(10)	P(15)	P(10)
Passing (Quarterbacks)						
Dropback		T(10)	P(10)	P(10)	*	*
Throw	T(10)	P(10)	P(10)	P(10)	P(10)	*
Drills	P(5)	P(15)	P(15)	P(5)	P(15)	P(10)

Activity	Practice Sessions					
	1	2	3	4	5	6
Receiving (Receivers and running backs)						
Routes		T(5)	T(5)	P(10)	P(10)	*
Catching	T(10)	P(10)	P(10)	P(10)	P(10)	P(10)
Drills	P(5)	P(10)	P(10)	P(15)	P(10)	P(10)
Kicking (Some activities for all, others position-specific)						
Kickoff		T(10)	P(5)	P(10)	P(5)	
Punt	T(10)	P(5)	P(5)		P(5)	
Field goal				T(10)	P(5)	P(5)
PAT						T(5)
Tackling (All defensive personnel)						
Form	T(10)	P(5)	P(5)			P(5)
Angle			T(5)	P(5)	P(5)	*
Straight		T(5)	P(5)	P(5)	*	*
Drills	P(5)	P(10)	P(10)	P(10)	P(10)	P(10)
Pass coverage (Linebackers and defensive backs)						
Footwork	T(10)	P(5)	P(5)	*	*	P(5)
Man-to-man		T(10)	P(10)	P(10)	P(10)	*
Zone					T(10)	P(10)
Drills	P(5)	P(10)	P(10)			
Scrimmage						
Small groups				P(15)	P(15)	P(20)
Full team						P(10)

(continued)

Activity	Practice Sessions					
	7	8	9	10	11	12
Warm-Up	P(10)	P(10)	P(10)	P(10)	P(10)	P(10)
Cool-Down	P(5)	P(5)	T(5)	P(5)	P(5)	P(5)
Evaluation	(5)	(5)	(5)	(5)	(5)	(5)
Stance	*	*	*	*	*	*
Blocking						
Drive	*	*	*	*	*	*
Downfield	*	*	*		*	*
Pass	*	*		*	*	*
Drills	P(10)	P(10)	P(15)	P(15)	P(10)	P(10)
Running						
Form			*	*	*	*
Starts	*	*	*	*	*	*
Drills		P(10)	P(15)	P(10)		
Passing						
Dropback	*	*		*	*	*
Throw	*	*	*	*	*	*
Drills	P(10)	P(10)	P(10)	P(15)		
Receiving						
Routes	*	*		*	*	*
Catching	*	*	*	*	*	
Drills	P(10)		P(10)	P(15)		

	Practice Sessions					
Activity	7	8	9	10	11	12
Kicking						
Kickoff	P10)		P(10)		*	*
Punt		P(10)		P(10)	*	*
Field goal		P(5)	P(5)	P(5)	*	*
PAT	P(5)		P(5)		*	*
Tackling						
Form	*	*	*	*	*	*
Angle	*	*	*	*	*	*
Straight	*	*	*	*	*	*
Drills		P(10)	P(10)	P(10)		
Pass coverage						
Footwork	*	P(5)	*	*	*	*
Man-to-man	P(5)	*	P(10)	*	*	*
Zone	*	P(10)		*	*	*
Drills			P(10)	P(25)	*	*
Scrimmage						
Small groups	P(20)	P(10)	P(20)	P(20)		
Full team	P(15)	P(20)	P(10)	P(10)	P(40)	P(50)

Appendix B

Common Football Officiating Signals

Time-out

Touchdown, field goal

Personal foul

Illegal use of hands

Illegal contact

Delay of game

Offside or encroaching

Holding

Illegal motion

First down

Pass interference

Incomplete pass, penalty
refused, missed kick

Failure to wear
required equipment

Flag guarding

Roughing kicker
or holder

Appendix C

Organizations to Contact for Coaching Children With Disabilities

American Athletic Association of the Deaf
3607 Washington Boulevard, Suite 4
Ogden, UT 84403-1737
(801) 393-8710
TTY: (801) 393-7916
Fax: (801) 393-2263

Disabled Sports USA
451 Hungerford Drive, Suite 100
Rockville, MD 20850
(301) 217-0960

Paralyzed Veterans of America
801 18th Street NW
Washington, DC 20006
(202) 872-1300
(800) 424-8200

Special Olympics International
1325 G Street NW, Suite 500
Washington, DC 20005
(202) 628-3630

U.S. Association of Blind Athletes
33 North Institute
Colorado Springs, CO 80903
(719) 630-0422

U.S. Cerebral Palsy Athletic Association
3810 West NW Highway, Suite 205
Dallas, TX 75220
(214) 351-1510

U.S. Les Autres Sports Association
1475 West Gray, Suite 166
Houston, TX 77019-4926
(713) 521-3737

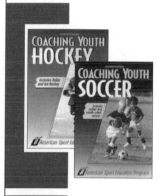

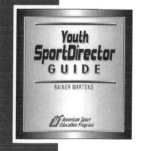

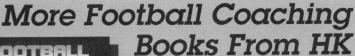

More Football Coaching Books From HK

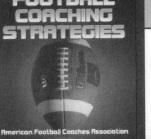

American Football Coaches Association

Foreword by Grant Teaff

1995 • Paper • 216 pp • Item PAFC0869
ISBN 0-87322-869-3 • $18.95 ($28.95 Canadian)

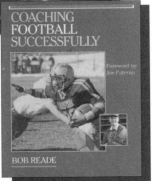

Bob Reade

Foreword by Joe Paterno

1994 • Paper • 192 pp
Item PREA0518 • ISBN 0-87322-518-X
$19.95 ($29.95 Canadian)

Dwight "Dee" Hawkes, Editor

Foreword by Dennis Erickson

1995 • Paper • 144 pp
Item PHAW0574 • ISBN 0-87322-574-0
$15.95 ($22.95 Canadian)

American Football Coaches Association

Foreword by Grant Teaff

1996 • Paper • 176 pp • Item PAFC0476
ISBN 0-88011-476-2 • $15.95 ($23.95 Canadian)

To place your book order, U.S. customers call
TOLL FREE 1-800-747-4457.
Customers outside the U.S. place your order
using the appropriate telephone
number/address shown in the front of this book.

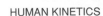

HUMAN KINETICS
The Premier Publisher for Sports & Fitness
http://www.humankinetics.com/

2335